Partnership Training
for Horse & Rider ®

IT'S ALL
ABOUT
Breakthroughs!

Partnership Training
for Horse & Rider

IT'S ALL
ABOUT
Breakthroughs!

**Hundreds of exercises that will make
you and your horse TRUE PARTNERS!**

*To Don,
Enjoy the journey!
Bob Jeffreys*

by Bob Jeffreys

The horse is the best animal there is;
no other has given man so much.
— BOB JEFFREYS

For Annette

ACKNOWLEDGEMENTS

I'd like to gratefully acknowledge the efforts of my wife, Annette, my good friends Kim and Enzo Taronji, Janine Fisher, and my partner, Suzanne Sheppard. Without their collective input and help, this book would not have been possible.

The crew. From left back row: Enzo Taronji (photographer), Annette Jeffreys (proofreader & wife), June Evers (Horse Hollow Press, Inc.), Suzanne Sheppard (business partner), Jessica Jeffreys (daughter), Jesse Holt (proofreader) and Janine Fisher (office manager); Lying down: Bob Jeffreys; In front: Kimia Taronji (ENKI Group)

MADE COMPLETELY IN THE U.S.A.
Copyright © 2004 by Bob Jeffreys & Horse Hollow Press, Inc.
Published by Horse Hollow Press, Inc. Goshen, NY, Phone: 800-4-1-HORSE
www.horsehollowpress.com • e-mail: info@horsehollowpress.com

Front and back cover photography: Nicki McManus
Photography courtesy Enzo & Kim Taronji, Michael Gold, Julie Petrick, Paula Peck and Janine Fisher
Editorial, design and illustrations: June Evers
Editorial arrangement: Jim Kersbergen
Proofreader and copy editor: Laura Pelner McCarthy, Silk Purse
Literary Agent Representation: ENKI Group, Ltd., PO Box 4644, Middletown, NY 10941

1st Printing: October 2004

Horse Hollow Press is not to be held responsible for any of the training tips in this book or how you apply them to your situation. We have deemed the exercises safe if used in accord with your trainer's recommendations and your own good judgement and common sense. Please realistically access your horsemanship skills and get the aid of a reputable trainer when needed. If you are afraid, then back up a few steps to the previous chapter. Your fear is telling you and quite possibly your horse are not ready to proceed.

ISBN: 0-9638814-7-7

Table of Contents

Table of Contents

Important Note

Horse Hollow Press is proud to present **It's All About Breakthroughs**. We're sure it'll greatly enhance the communication and performance between you and your horse.

As with all aspects of horse care and training, the exercises within this book require care, caution and patience on your part. Bob Jeffreys is an accomplished horseman of over 40 years with countless hours of teaching, training, education and experience behind him. Realistically assess your own skills and your horse's training level and ability before attempting any of these exercises. Best of all, if possible, try to attend a Bob Jeffreys clinic.

Most importantly, follow the sequence of lessons and exercises outlined by the author in the Table of Contents. There is a logic to the order that directly relates to your horse's learning and his responsiveness to your commands. And, truly, follow your gut. If you are afraid, then back up a few steps to the previous chapter. Your fear is telling you and quite possibly your horse are not ready to proceed.

Bob also repeatedly recommends you work with a lunge line or lead rope. Please obey all horseman's common sense rules of basic lead rope use and never wrap anything around your hands, fingers or arms. Remember to use appropriate protective gear for your horse and Horse Hollow Press *always* recommends a helmet for yourself.

With these recommendations in mind, it is our pleasure to share with you these fabulous partnership-gaining exercises. And have fun learning to become your horse's true partner.

—Horse Hollow Press, Inc.

Bob Jeffreys and his partner, Blackjac.

Foreword

My wife, Kimia, and I met Bob Jeffreys back in 1994. At that time, we were both in our thirties and just starting to rekindle our love for horses and riding.

Before the establishment of his training facility (Jeffcrest Ranch), Bob was training horses and riders at a ranch that offered guided trail rides in a nearby park. Kimia and I had heard about this place from some friends and we made plans to go for a nice trail ride one beautiful summer day. We drove for almost two hours to get there, but because of weekend traffic coming out of New York City, we arrived late and we missed the ride by a few minutes. The owner would not let us rent horses and go out on our own (and rightly so, as he didn't know us very well and knew nothing of our riding abilities). We thought our day ruined, and started thinking of less enjoyable alternatives when Bob approached us and offered to take the two of us out on a ride. We had no idea of who he was, but who cared! We were just happy to go out riding.

Even though taking out trail rides was not part of his work as a trainer, Bob took time out of his busy schedule to salvage our weekend. He helped us get our horses ready, loaded them onto his trailer with his own horse, Eagle (the most beautiful blue-eyed pinto I'd ever seen), and drove us all in his personal pickup truck to the nearby state park. That day we had the most enjoyable trail ride of our lives. Bob quietly observed our riding capabilities without being judgmental and then, ever so gently, gauged the ride and the terrain so both my wife and I would both have a great experience.

As the day progressed, my wife and I became more and more inquisitive about Bob's background. Bob answered all the questions we threw at him and gave us advice when asked. We started realizing that this was not your average ranch hand. This guy really knew what he was talking about and he dispensed his knowledge in a kind, gentle manner that made us very comfortable. Not only that, this was the first time that we were listening to someone that actually made sense. There was no "mystical" blabber or highbrow terminology meant to intimidate us into thinking we were talking to some supreme horse being. Just good old-fashioned English and "baby step" explanations that tied it all together.

That day in the park I learned more about riding and horses than in over thirty years of advice, expensive lessons and publications.

At the end of the day, we returned to the ranch and paid the owner for the "rental" horses. I then offered Bob payment for his services but he refused to take any money from us. He just shook our hands and said it was a pleasure riding with us and he would love to do it again.

That day, in a way, summarizes what Bob Jeffreys is all about. Bob trains people and horses in a kind, non-judgmental, efficient and straightforward way that is not pretentious and does not make you feel insecure. He speaks in plain English and his training, like his cues to a horse, is clear and simple. His goal is to improve the rider-horse partnership and the enjoyment you get out of it.

Over the past eight years Bob has become much more than our trainer. He is our best friend. Kim and I have watched his popularity grow based on his great reputation (I guess we are not the only good judges of talent) and the development of his Partnership Training System. Bob has carried us through some rough horse-related times, and we are happy to say that he has been there for all the breakthroughs. We are extremely lucky that he came into our lives when he did.

In the year 2000 my wife and I moved into our dream

house. We built Monte Cristo Ranch as a small private horse facility for our family to enjoy our horses. And it is one mile down the road from Jeffcrest Ranch! I wish you could all be as lucky as we are and have Bob "down the road a bit" when you have horse questions or issues to resolve with your equine partner. But since you don't, this training manual is the next best thing.

I know you will enjoy working with Bob and his Partnership Training System. I hope your experience will be as rich and rewarding as ours has been.

Enzo "Doc" Taronji

P.S. Eagle is now my horse. I talked Bob into letting me have him four years ago and with Bob's help and training system, I have formed a bond with this horse to a level I never thought possible. As far as I'm concerned, Eagle and I have the perfect Partnership! ❧

A special thanks to my business partner, Suzanne Sheppard, for keeping this project alive and working on its development in so many ways.

Preface

Over the years, the most often repeated suggestion from my clinic participants and Trainer Education Program students was to make available a written version of my philosophies and teaching methods. This project was initiated primarily in response to those requests. People kept telling me that after using my methods, they were able to achieve noticeable breakthroughs in their training and began to achieve a real partnership with their horses.

Taking their comments and requests seriously, I embarked on writing this book so *everyone* working on these exercises and lessons would see important and readily noticeable changes in their understanding of horses and how they learn. Sometimes even the realization of "Hey, I didn't know that!" is a breakthrough in itself.

The sequential and progressive nature of the lessons is designed to keep things easy for your horse and safe for you. If you can take your time and do the lessons correctly, your very own breakthroughs will add up and you, too, will be well on your way to building that perfect partnership with your horse.

Bob Jeffreys on Blackjac at Equine Affaire in Ohio.

About Bob Jeffreys

Bob began riding in his childhood on Staten Island, New York over 40 years ago. He earned a BBA degree from St. John's University and after college, he went to work in the oil business where he ultimately became the president of the U.S. division of a foreign-owned trading company. He has traveled nationally and internationally dealing with people of diverse backgrounds and cultures. As technology reduced the social part of his work, Bob followed what he describes as a higher calling. No matter where he was, he always seemed to wind up at the local barn working with both horse owners and their horses. Making the career change was a natural choice. This prompted him to start Jeffcrest Ranch, his own training and riding instruction facility in Middletown, New York.

Bob's considerable years of experience and his work with many well-known trainers and thousands of horses have led him to develop **The Partnership Training for Horse & Rider®** system which encompasses the most effective techniques yet devised. His system enhances the rider's understanding of why horses do what they do and how it's best to communicate with them by gaining control over their specific parts. He teaches people to analyze whether the horse is afraid or confused and how to deal with each situation. Bob's methods focus on helping the horse to succeed rather than testing him to failure. This results in a far more willing equine partner.

Bob writes a monthly column for N.Y. Horse. He has been published in American Farriers Journal, Equine Journal, Infohorse.com and many, many other equine publications. He

Above: Bob on Blackjac and Suzanne Sheppard on Lukka, her Icelandic horse, in sync over a tarp at Equine Affaire, Ohio.

Above: Bob teaches at one of his clinics.

and his business partner, Suzanne Sheppard, have been guests on TV and radio shows, including an interview on the nationally known Rick Lamb's Horse Show. They have been headliners and presenters at such prestigious events as Equine Affaire (in Ohio and Massachussetts), Equine Event East (in Virginia), Georgia Horse Fair, Northeast Horseman's Conference, International Centered Riding® Symposium and many more. Additionally, they have given hundreds of clinics all over the country to thousands of people.

While he loves traveling to the hundreds of events and teaching, his favorite program is his very own **Trainer Education Program** where he spends 6 weeks each year at Jeffcrest Ranch working with 8 - 10 dedicated and devoted horse people who truly want to learn all that they can about horses and their training.

Above: Bob and Lucky, a registered Paint.

Partnership Training
for Horse & Rider

PHASE 1

Ground & Under-Saddle Foundation Exercises

Part•ner•ship: *noun*, a relationship...usually involving close cooperation between parties having specified and joint rights and responsibilities.

—MERRIAM-WEBSTER'S COLLEGIATE DICTIONARY

Introduction

TREAT YOUR HORSE AS A WILLING
PARTNER AND YOU'LL GET ONE

I teach a form of horsemanship that I call **Partnership Training for Horse & Rider.** This term is threefold in meaning: PART—PARTNER—PARTNERSHIP. I'll show you how to gain control over various individual parts of the horse which makes it easier to control the whole horse. I'll explain why you should treat your horse as your partner, not your pet, and to employ riding techniques that are designed to take your partnership to a level beyond that which you thought possible.

Hopefully you will note that a constant theme runs throughout this book. It is simply that we must always help our horse to succeed rather than test him to failure.

This is accomplished by breaking all our lessons into baby steps. By consistently giving your horse tasks that do not overwhelm him, you'll build his confidence. He gets used to doing things correctly and being praised for it rather than doing something wrong (to us) and being punished. You build a solid foundation upon which to teach the more difficult or advanced maneuvers. In human terms, it's the equivalent of teaching a child simple math before attempting algebra.

Horses and humans are two very different species just trying to find some common ground on which to walk. Physical differences are obvious. Horses are bigger, stronger and faster than we are. This fact is a crucial reason why we must consider them our partners and not pets (you don't want your horse jumping on your lap or nibbling on your clothes no matter how "cute" you might think this is when they're babies!).

Just as importantly, however, is the fact that horses are prey animals and we are predators. Danger causes horses to

Bob Jeffreys (left) and Suzanne Sheppard (above).

flee and people to fight — opposite reactions. Having their eyes set on the side of their heads gives them great peripheral vision, but less depth perception than humans. Conversely, we have eyes in the front of our heads which gives us great depth perception, but relatively poor peripheral vision. The horse's bilateral vision allows him to see approaching predators, while our binocular vision gives us the ability to judge distances and catch things. Again, it appears we're on opposite ends of the spectrum.

> **BOB SAYS:**
> Any horse of any age with any amount of training will benefit from the exercises in this book.

When we understand why our horse sometimes gets anxious (he may see or hear something we don't), or is afraid to cross a stream that's only three inches deep (to him it may look like the abyss), we can figure out a way to deal with these and other situations.

Horses are herd animals. Their safety and their very survival are linked to the rest of the herd and its leader. When the leader says run, they run. If the leader says it's O.K. to graze, they graze. The members of the herd don't question the leader because they trust him. We need to become the leader of our two-animal herd. We need to be the proactive or "thinking" partner in our relationship because we have been blessed with

BOB SAYS:
When you ask your horse to do something, you need to get out of his way and let him do it.

a higher intelligence than our equine friends. We also need to get out of the horse's way, once we've made a request, and allow him to perform the task without interference. Our horse is a natural for the reactive or "doer" role since he is blessed with physical attributes far superior to our own.

While it's nice that we've defined our respective roles in our partnership, we still have to convince our horse that we should be the leader. In order to do this, we're going to have to act a little bit more like another horse would. Now, don't worry, you don't have to crawl around on all fours or sleep standing up, but you will have to ask certain things from your horse that an alpha horse might ask. Move, move a little faster, or move your hindquarters over or back up when I ask you to. The catch here is that there are ways to do this which could cause your horse to be wary of you or even to be afraid of you; we are not interested in these ways. There is, however, another fun way to become the alpha partner or leader that would not only place us higher in the pecking order, but also serve to gain our horse's trust and show him we won't hurt him. We'll cover the specifics later, but for now, I just want to introduce you to the **"Vowel Method of Applied Pressure."**

BOB SAYS:
Use pressure instead of force to achieve the desired goal.

Whether you're on the ground or in the saddle, you'll need to use some form of pressure to make a request of your horse.

The **Vowel Method** teaches you to use as little as possible but always as much as you need. "A.E.I.O.U." as applied to pressure stands for **ASK, ENCOURAGE, INSIST, ORDER** and **UNDO.** You must always start with "A" and always end with "U." What you use in between "Ask" and "Undo" is determined by your horse.

Although it is initially important to praise your horse when he gets something right, remember that horses are not motivated so much by kind words, treats or even petting. These are things we desire. Our horses want safety, comfort and consistency in our release of pressure when they perform our requests. They will, in time, draw their own consistency from us. If we act out the role of lead horse, our requests will seem more natural for our horse to understand.

"Natural horsemanship" is a common term these days, but we must understand that it does not mean that horses should be allowed to do whatever comes natural to them. To me, natural horsemanship is the art of using the horse's natural characteristics in order to teach him to respond in a conditioned manner to natural stimuli or to a human request. What is natural to a horse when he is frightened is to spin around and bolt away from the danger, whether real or perceived. This is not a reaction that we desire and may even be dangerous. While we cannot teach a horse not to be afraid, we can condition him so that his natural reaction to fear is altered in the beginning to one of stopping his feet and facing that which scared him. We'll cover the "how to" part of this in the section on spook-proofing your horse.

> **BOB SAYS:**
> Release pressure the instant your horse complies with your request. This tells him "Thanks, that was the right answer"

> **BOB SAYS:**
> Work with your horse's natural trait of laziness.

Another natural trait is laziness. Horses, not unlike humans, are lazy by nature (now don't take this personally, just follow me for a second). They would prefer to spend their day grazing in the pasture or playing with the other horses rather than cantering circles or sidepassing under saddle.

Our human preferences would have us riding our horse rather than working because even a not-so-good day of riding is better than any day at work. My oldest son, Ryan, once told

The Vowel Method of Applying Pressure

A	**ASK** as gently as possible to perform a task, wait two seconds
E	If he doesn't respond, **ENCOURAGE** with a tad more pressure, wait two seconds
I	Then **INSIST** with a little more, wait two seconds
O	**ORDER** with as much pressure as you need
U	Once your horse has accomplished the task, **UNDO** all pressure

me to start working smarter, not harder. We can use this trait of laziness (thus working smarter not harder) to teach our horses to stand still while we mount or to stop when we ask them to. Again, it should be noted that you cannot make a horse stand still or stop; they are far too big and strong to be out-muscled by us. Any device that you use on him, like more severe bits or mechanical hackamores, only forces him to accept more pain, and eventually he will get used to it, brace against it and run through it.

An old cowboy saying agrees, stating that "You can't make a horse stop, but you can surely make him wish he had." I'd like to take it to a higher level by actually making it the horse's own desire, or his idea, to stop or stand still. Instead of fighting with the horse that won't stop, move him faster and farther

BOB SAYS:
Make it your horse's desire to stop.

than he would like to go and then offer an opportunity to stop. If he ignores it, move him faster again. Keep repeating until he actually wants to stop. It becomes his idea that stopping or standing still is a good thing.

When he does stop, let him enjoy the stop, pet him and let him rest for at least three seconds. It would be easier to teach your horse this "stopping" lesson or the "stand still" lesson after you've ridden awhile. Your horse may be tired and will learn it faster.

Think about this in human terms. You wake up in the morning, refreshed and full of energy. You're ready to take on the world, but your boss tells you to sit in a chair and wait for further instructions. You'd probably feel a little anxious and bored. But if you had to off-load five hundred bales of hay and stack them in the barn first, that chair might start to look a whole lot better.

In summary, the following text will show you how to gain your horse's trust, how to condition him to say "yes" to your requests, and how important it is to consistently release any applied pressure when he responds. You'll be presented with the knowledge and the tools required to teach your horse without having to resort to chains, whips, harsh bits, tie downs or any other "corrective" devices.

You'll be prepared, together with your partner, to enjoy your very own breakthroughs! ⚘

Above: Use a ten- or twelve-foot cotton lead for this exercise. I never use lead ropes that contain any form of chain as chains cause pain and pain is never a good motivator.

Gaining Trust
THE MOST IMPORTANT THING IN YOUR HORSE'S LIFE IS HIS SAFETY. HE WON'T LEARN ANYTHING WITHOUT IT

We'll start to gain our horse's trust while we're safely on the ground. Assuming your horse will accept a halter, we'll attach a ten or twelve-foot lead rope made of cotton, as it is easier on your hands if your horse tries to pull away. Also, I never use lead ropes that contain any form of chain as chains cause pain and pain is never a good motivator.

Take your horse to an enclosed corral or arena that he's comfortable with. Our first goal for this lesson is to touch or rub our horse with our hands all over his body. We do this in order to show our horse that we won't hurt him and that he doesn't need to protect any areas of his body from us.

We'll start with the large areas like his neck, barrel and rump and then proceed to more sensitive

BOB SAYS:
Your older horse will really appreciate it when you take the time (in this **Gaining Trust** section) to get to know him well.

*If your horse is uncomfortable with an area on his body, use the **approach and retreat method** (see page 30) to gain his trust. It is important to work this uneasiness out completely before proceeding.*

29

areas like his ears, legs, flank area and even up under the tail head. Make sure you can touch his belly, inside the legs, etc. Rub your horse, don't tickle him or slap him. If you encounter any resistance, or if your horse flinches as you try to touch a certain spot, use the "approach and retreat" method to overcome this anxiety.

> **BOB SAYS:**
> Use the **approach and retreat method**, whenever your horse seems uncomfortable with your touch on any part of his body.

This is where you start to act a little more like a horse. When horses see something new, they may at first snort, back up, raise their heads or even run away. But if they're not chased by the object, they will come back to investigate it further, coming a little closer to it each time they approach. They approach and retreat from the new object until comfortable with it.

The perfect story to demonstrate this happened when I was working with my tractor in a pasture behind a run-in shed.

> **BOB SAYS:**
> Don't ever tickle or slap him!

The rear tire fell off. A few of the resident horses eventually appeared around the corner, saw that tractor leaning over on its side, snorted, backed away quickly and finally turned and ran. I assumed it would be safe to leave the tractor there until the next day when I could get some help to right it.

Well, the next morning when I returned, those horses had removed all the rubber from the pedals, pulled the ball off the gear levers, and were playing a form of football with the seat!

They approach to see if it's safe, but retreat to make sure. Slowly, little by little, they'll go up to the object. When they're absolutely sure it's safe, it's time to play with it.

Humans, on the other hand, when seeing something for the first time, walk right up to it, touch it, push or kick it and maybe even take it apart and try to put it back together again.

So, if your horse is uncomfortable when you touch his flank, go back to rubbing your hand on his neck and barrel, come toward the flank, stop short of it, and go back to the neck. Repeat while coming one inch or so closer to the flank area each time. Finally, just quickly stroke the flank and return

Left: It's important that we not approach the ear like we're going to do something bad. The horse will sense our apprehension and become afraid.

to the neck. Eventually, you can slow down your hand speed while rubbing the flank until he's no longer concerned.

Another area that horses sometimes don't want us near is their ears. Start rubbing between his eyes, then move your hand 1 inch towards his ears and then go back to between his eyes. Remain near his ears only a short period of time. Now go 1 1/2 inches closer towards one of his ears and back again. Then 2 inches, etc. When you are finally ready to touch his ear, move your hand swiftly and completely over the ear. He might be a little upset but the deed's already been done. Repeat this procedure and begin to move your hand more slowly, causing it to remain on your horse's ear longer each time. Finally, you'll be able to stroke it gently from front to back and eventually pet inside the ear.

BOB SAYS:
Don't rush this **Gaining Trust** section, it is very important for the future lessons in this book.

When he is comfortable with you touching his whole body, start asking him to take a little weight off each leg one at a time as a precursor to picking up his feet.

Don't rush this part of your training. It's imperative that your horse trust you to touch any part of his body. If he doesn't, that "hole" in his training will show up later. It could be that he won't trust you enough to cross a stream or to go away from his stable mates.

Our next goal is to teach our horse to move away from

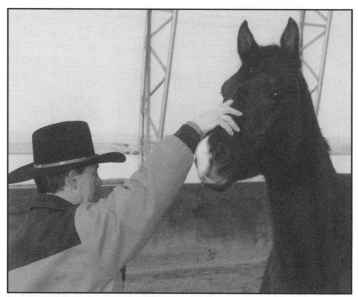

Above and left: Add a tad of pressure to his nose to ask your horse to back up. Below: Release the pressure the instant he starts to move backwards.

BOB SAYS:
Always start with the "ASK" of the **Vowel Method** if you want a more responsive horse.

The Importance of the "Release"

The only way a horse "knows" for sure he gave you the correct response is by the *immediate* release of pressure! Pressure can be from the lead rope, rein or leg pressure. It can even be a mean face (see page 44). Releasing the pressure says, "Thank you, partner, that's what I wanted."

pressure. Most people believe horses move away from pressure naturally, but this is not the case. The truth is horses, just like people, naturally move into pressure in order to stay balanced. We have to alter this natural tendency and condition them to move away from pressure.

Start by standing in front of your horse. Place a hand on the bridge of his nose and add just a tad of pressure to ask him to back up. He'll probably try to avoid you by taking his head up, down or sideways at first, so be ready and stay with him. In this way, you'll avoid releasing during the undesirable, evasive behavior, which would only reinforce the wrong response! You might need to increase the pressure by pushing harder with your hand to the "**encourage**," "**insist**," or even the "**order**" phase, but the instant he starts to move backwards "**undo**" the pressure and pet the horse. Don't assume you must get to a particular stage before he'll move; you must always start with the "**ask**" phase if you expect your horse to become more responsive. Your horse should get better and better and much more responsive as he starts to understand what you want.

Now place one hand on his shoulder and the other hand on the side of his jaw while you're facing his neck. You'll have to work on both sides, so it doesn't matter which side you start with. Apply pressure with both hands until he moves his front end one step over to the side. Be sure to undo your pressure to reward the correct response. You can gradually build up to two steps, three steps, etc., until you can complete

In this series of photos (this page and next page), you can see how my body position pushes the horse's front end around to the right with his hind end remaining relatively still.

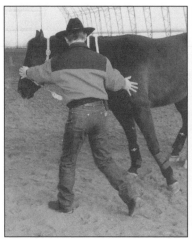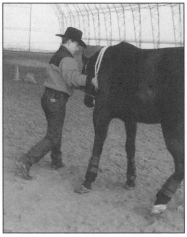

Above and right: Continued from the photo on page 33. Here I am completing a turn on the hindquarters. I start with the "ASK," and "UNDO" as soon as he moves where I want him to.

a full turn on the hindquarters (the front end moving around while the hind end remains relatively still). Remember to apply pressure according to the **Vowel Method.**

Next, we can ask the hindquarters to move while the front end remains relatively still (turn on the forehand, photos upper right). Start by facing the left side of your horse near the barrel. While using the lead rope in your left hand gently pull his head toward you and push on his barrel with your right hand until he moves over in the direction of your push. When you push his barrel, pick a spot where you'd place your leg while riding to cue him to move his hindquarters. Use as little push as possible, but, once again, add pressure gradually until the rear legs move to the side. When they do, undo the pressure, but rub your horse before completely removing your hand. In this way, he won't try to run away from your hand as you approach, but only move away from it when you ask him to. Repeat the procedure on the other side of your horse.

Now let's place our right hand on top of the horse's head and our left hand on the bridge of his nose while standing on his left side. Ask with a little pressure from both hands for him to both lower his head and bring it over to the left. Undo the pressure on any movement in the desired direction. If your horse doesn't respond, just wait awhile before slightly increasing your

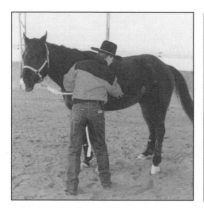 

Above and right: Here, I am giving the hindquarters the cue to move away while the front end remains still. Whenever you make your horse move, it confirms you as the leader.

pressure. However, if your horse shows active resistance (i.e., he takes his head upward) do not release, but do not add more pressure at this point; simply maintain your current level of pressure until he moves his head in the desired direction and then undo. The reason we don't add more pressure on this particular lesson is that we don't want to ask the horse to go against his instincts at this point in our training. If we did, we'd be inviting a fight.

Above: This is the starting position: Place your right hand on the top of the horse's head and the left hand on the bridge of his nose. Right: Ahhh! Here the horse is in the perfect position!

Repeat until every time you ask he'll drop his head 3-6 inches downward and also bring it 3-6 inches over to the side. When he will do this every time you request it, work on the most sensitive parts of the head. Start rubbing his nose and inside his mouth gently; then add one finger into his mouth in the place where the bit would lie. Add another finger or two until he opens his mouth. In addition to gaining trust, we're preparing him for eventual bridling.

We can also try to lead our horse with just our hand cupped under or around his chin. Take your time and be patient, but if you've done all the preceding work your horse should catch on in just a few minutes. If, however, he tries to evade you, use the halter to hold onto him until he begins to move.

When we have finished this lesson, we should have the ability to move our horse backwards, forwards, front end over and back end over, all with just our hands. We will have made great strides toward gaining his trust and we have already planted the seed in his mind that we are causing him to perform these movements. We are becoming his friend, his partner, his leader. Now we will need to repeat all the above movements with the halter and lead rope. ❧

BOB SAYS:
For this particular lesson, teaching your horse to lower his head, it is important not to increase pressure via the **Vowel Method**, but to maintain pressure to achieve your goal and release on the tiniest downward movement of your horse's head.

BOB SAYS:
Repeat this section with the halter and lead rope as an extension of your hand as well.

Breakthrough!

Sacking Out
DESENSITIZE YOUR HORSE TO THE
OBJECTS HE ENCOUNTERS EVERY DAY

"**Sacking out**" simply means getting your horse used to objects that he'll encounter on a daily basis. The first object was our hands and now we'll use a rope. Begin in a small corral or round pen. Outfit your horse with a halter and lead rope held loosely. This will give you something to hold on to should your horse try to leave.

*Above: This is where we use the **approach & retreat** method to accomplish our goal. We're telling the horse that if he'll accept this rope at 10 feet away for just a few seconds, we'll remove this pressure and leave. Here I am letting the horse investigate the rope. I'm not shoving it in his face.*

Now stand in front of your horse about 10 feet or so and hold a rolled up lariat (or lunge line) in your hand. Approach the horse and gently show him the lariat by holding it about one foot in front of his nose. Let him look at it and sniff it before you retreat. If he takes off or is highly excited, stop him by adding pressure on the lead rope attached to his halter. Start over again, but show him the rope from 10 feet away, then 9 feet, 8 feet, etc., until you can walk right up to him with it.

Approach again, let him sniff it and then pet the front of his face between his eyes with

BOB SAYS:
This is great for older trained horses. You'd be surprised how many so called "broke" horses are not comfortable with a rope or lunge line.

Above: We have started to acquaint the horse with the feel of the rope gently landing on him. You should not "hit" him with the rope.

the rope and retreat again. Approach, rub his face and now his neck before retreating. Complete this process with the rope until you can touch any part of his body with it.

Now, start to gently toss the lead rope over his withers, back, rump and eventually both his front and back legs. The rope should just be "landing" on the horse; you should not "hit" him with the rope. As always, do everything from both sides. This exercise will teach your horse to accept minor bumps such as your leg brushing his rump when you mount or a tree branch contacting his body on the trail.

Finally, put that coiled up rope on top of your horse's head around both ears. If you can't do this it's a sign that your horse isn't comfortable with something either above him or on his

Above: As you can see, this horse is not bothered by the rope on his head and around his ears.

BOB SAYS:
If you can't put something on or above your horse's head, he's not yet safe to ride.

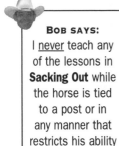
head, and he's not yet safe to ride. Keep playing with him until that rope no longer bothers him.

You can now move on and repeat all these sacking out steps with the saddle blanket. Begin by approaching with the blanket folded up so that it approximates the size of the coiled rope. When you can touch him all over with the folded blanket, open it halfway up (while standing at least five feet in front of the horse so he sees what you are doing and doesn't get scared or strike at the blanket) and sack him out all over.

Finally, open the blanket fully, put it around the cinch area and pull up (simulating the feel of a saddle cinch), throw it over his back, rump, neck, and head and drop it off both sides to the ground. When we can accomplish all this and our horse remains calm, he is sacked out and we're ready to move on. ❧

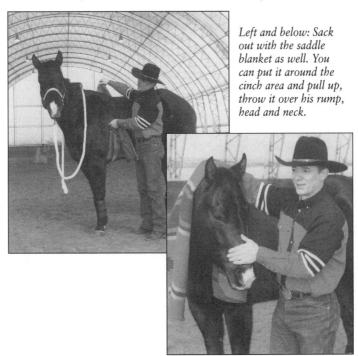

Left and below: Sack out with the saddle blanket as well. You can put it around the cinch area and pull up, throw it over his rump, head and neck.

Some folks think this term refers to keeping things natural for the horse, letting him do what he wants to do, instead of what we want him to do. This is not how I'd like to define "natural horsemanship." I define it as using the "natural" traits of the horse in order to teach him conditioned responses.

One example would be the horse's natural trait of laziness. It's natural for all animals to be lazy.

Let's use that natural trait to make our horse stop. I like to tell people that you really can't force a horse to stop. A horse weighs on average about 1200 pounds. Horses are so much stronger, faster and quicker than we are that if they don't want to stop, we really can't make them. I'm talking here about normal riding and normal bits. There are cruel methods out there, but that's NOT our goal. Our goal is to become our horse's partner.

So let's offer our horse a chance to stop. Let's say we're doing some walking, trotting or loping exercises, we ask him to stop and he says, "Nope! I'm just going to keep going!" Then, whatever gait I'm in, I'm going to ask him to go a little bit faster and a little bit farther and then, I'm going to keep him going. When he wants to slow down, I'm going to say, "No! You can't. I want you to go farther and faster." Then, after I've pushed him longer than he wanted to go, and faster than he wanted to go, I'm going to offer him a chance to stop. If he doesn't take it, then we'll go faster than before and longer than before. We might even change directions from where he wants to go. Then, I'll offer him another chance to stop. And, if he still says no, well, we'll continue the exercise until he gets the message that stopping is a really, really good idea.

So next time you ask him to stop, he'll say, "Oh, I thought you'd never ask!" Then you can let him enjoy the stop. I always want my horses to enjoy their stops. I want to actually make stopping fun for him and have it become his idea to stop, but not until I tell him. And I want him to look forward to stopping.

To me, that is what natural horsemanship is all about.

Follow the Feel

TEACH HIM TO LEAD EASILY
AND STAND STILL WHILE TIED

We can now begin to teach our horse to follow the "feel" or the pull of the rope so that he will be easy to lead and won't pull back when tied. Some of the worst accidents occur when horses pull back when tied. They can panic, breaking boards, halters, the rope or cross-ties. They might even break their own necks, so spend some time here to help your horse stay safe.

First, we need to distinguish between a pull and a jerk. Quick little snaps, jerks or bumps with the lead rope teach nothing and are extremely annoying to your horse. Please don't ever jerk on your horse's lead rope or reins if you want him to trust you as a fair leader.

> **BOB SAYS:**
> Don't ever jerk on your horse's lead rope or reins if you want him to trust you as a fair leader!

Rather, take the slack out of the rope slowly allowing him to respond on your "ask." If, however, you remove all the slack and your horse still doesn't yield, just add more pressure (pulling harder, but not faster) and keep adding pressure gradually until you get the desired movement.

You may initially have to move beyond "ask" to "encourage," "insist" or even "order" (review the **Vowel Method** on page 26), but you "undo" the instant he gives you movement in the direction requested. In this manner, you'll eventually get your horse lighter and always responding on just the "ask."

> **BOB SAYS:**
> Horses are prey animals and hate to be held tightly. If you want him to stand quietly, hold the lead with slack in the rope.

Let's begin by asking the horse to follow the pull of the rope by stepping towards it rather than pulling back against it. Using your 10-12 foot lead rope, face your horse's left shoulder and back away until you're about 8-

41

Above: I'm starting to ask the horse to turn to his left. I am asking him to fol-low the feel.

Right: Even with slack in the lead, he has started to turn towards me as if to ask, "Yes, what can I do for you now?" This is the lightness we always look for.

Left: Here you can see that as my left hand is approaching the horse's left shoul-der point, he is already starting to back. Again, we are experienc-ing the lightness we look for.

10 feet off to his side. Using the **Vowel Method**, slowly take out the slack and add pressure until he turns toward you. Release and reward with a good rub. Repeat until he's really light and then do the lesson from the right side.

In this next phase, we'll teach your horse to go backwards. Stand 5-8 feet in front of the horse, facing him while holding the lead rope in your hands. Walk toward your horse's left shoulder point and adjust your rope so that when your body arrives at the shoulder point, all the slack will have been removed. As you continue to walk, you'll start to apply pressure to your horse's nose (via the halter) until he steps backwards. Then "undo" and pet.

> **BOB SAYS:**
> Pet your horse to let him know he's succeeded. They do understand.

Do this from both sides until your horse will back up willingly and lightly. If your horse seems totally confused, use a mean face and an aggressive posture (stand up as tall as you can and puff up your chest in an exaggerated fashion) while coming toward him until he understands that he should back up.

Finally, we need to teach our horse to come to us when we invite him. Stand 8-10 feet in front of your horse with the lead rope lying on the ground between you and where it hooks to the halter ring. Make a happy face, use a friendly posture and slow-

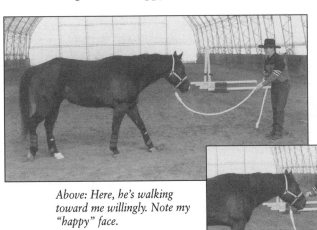

Above: Here, he's walking toward me willingly. Note my "happy" face.

Right: Then, I say "thanks for coming over" with a rub.

43

ly take up the slack until he moves towards you. Again, use the **Vowel Method** to apply the necessary pressure, then undo and praise when he moves forward. The happy face and friendly posture will encourage him to come toward you just as the mean face and aggressive posture (which is also a form of pressure) helped him to understand he should move away from you.

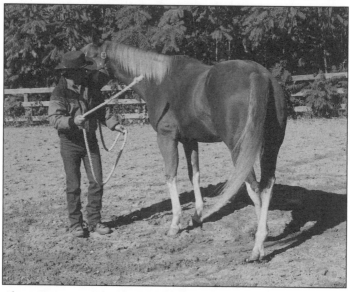

Above: To start to disengage the hindquarters, I stare at the horse's hip while I twirl the end of my lead rope right at the hip (more pressure) to get some movement. Note how the horse is starting to cross over behind; this is the beginning of disengaging the hip. Yes! I simply stare at his hip to put pressure on the hip. Horses are incredibly sensitive creatures and can actually feel that stare.

The Power of the Happy and Mean Face

Horses are masters of body language. When they were foals, their mothers invited them to come close with a happy and loving look. When they wanted the foals to move away, they chased them with a nasty look or even a nip. Your horse very definitely reads your facial expressions!

You can use the mean face as a form of pressure to get your horse to move away from you. And, likewise, use the happy face to bring him towards you.

Right: He has begun to disengage his hindquarters. Note the determined expression I am using. Horses can sense that determination in your expression; it's the power of the mean face.

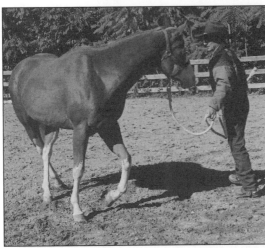

Left: Here you see the first step to the side. His hindquarters are disengaged and his forward motion is stopped.

What is "Disengage the Hindquarters"?

Since the hindquarters are effectively the engine of the horse, when you disengage this engine or move his rear legs sideways, you inhibit forward motion. This action is reminiscent of the way in which an experienced downhill skier will turn at the hips to end his run. This movement also encourages the horse to switch off the reactive side of his brain and engages the "thinking" side by forcing him to focus on you!

If our horse decides to bolt, buck or run away, we can disengage the hips as soon as one of these behaviors occurs and stop it.

That mean face and aggressive posture are also useful when asking the horse to disengage his hindquarters. Hold the lead rope about 5-6 feet from the buckle in one hand and twirl the other end of it with your other hand at the hip. When he moves his hip over undo all your pressure and praise him.

To make absolutely sure our horse knows he's to **follow the feel** of the rope, use a 30-foot lariat or lunge line and attach it to his halter. While holding the other end, wrap the rope around the right side of your horse, behind his rump, and stand off about 6-8 feet to the left side of his rump. He will see you with his left eye, but as you slowly take the slack out of the rope, he'll feel the pull from the right side and should follow it all the way around to the right until he's facing you. Repeat on the other side.

When your horse is responding nicely to this exercise, you can start tying your horse.

BOB SAYS:
If our horse does not respond to the "follow the feel" exercise, see photo, he is not yet safe to tie!

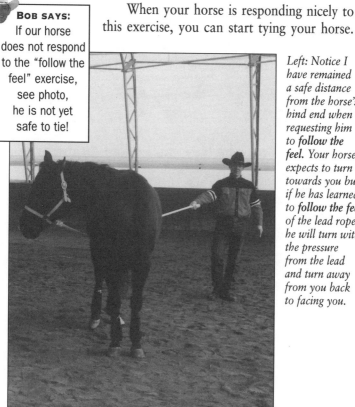

*Left: Notice I have remained a safe distance from the horse's hind end when requesting him to **follow the feel**. Your horse expects to turn towards you but if he has learned to **follow the feel** of the lead rope, he will turn with the pressure from the lead and turn away from you back to facing you.*

Just wrap the lead rope several times around a post without making a knot. Let him stand tied for only five minutes, but gradually build over a month's time to at least an hour.

If in the beginning he pulls back, the rope will simply unwind and your horse will not get hurt or panic. This action of pulling back however, will tell you that you need more work on **following the feel.** As you tie for longer periods of time,

don't react to his pawing or moving side to side or crying out to buddies. These are all normal attempts by our horse to inform us that he would rather be elsewhere. We must not yell at him to stop because it would be giving him the attention he is seeking. Wait until he's standing quietly before untying him. This untying will then be seen as a reward for doing the right thing. Eventually the horse will learn to be patient and even enjoy the "down" time. ❧

Bob on a Conditioned Response in Horses

If I approached somebody who I just met for the first time and I extended my hand, he probably would extend his hand in return. We'd shake hands and introduce ourselves. If he didn't shake my hand, I'd consider it rude because we, as Americans, have been conditioned to respond by shaking hands in an introduction to someone new.

It's the same when I pick up the lead rope — I expect my horse to yield to it as if responding to me with a "Yes, what can I do for you now?" And, when I pick up the right rein, I expect him to give his head to the right and wait for me to make such a request. He needs to answer that call from me because it's a conditioned response he will have learned. It's also a sign of respect.

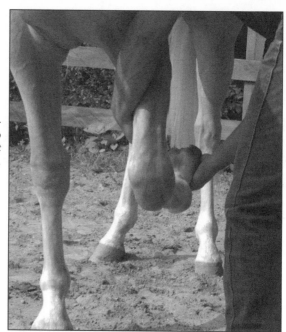

Right: The correct position to pick up a left front leg.

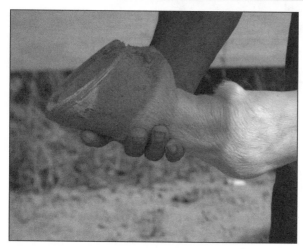

Left: Cup the foot gently, do not grab or hold it tightly. He won't fear being trapped.

Picking Up His Feet
HIS FOOT SHOULD NOT WEIGH ANYTHING
WHILE YOU'RE HOLDING IT

If you've ever wondered why a horse might be reluctant to give you his feet, remember that he is a prey animal. The act of letting someone hold a foot prevents him from fleeing from danger. Think about it from the horse's perspective. A predator (us) tries to grab his foot so he can't get away, or tries to pull a foot out from under him causing him to fall, threatening his life. But, by this point in this book, we've done all of our homework from the previous chapters. Our horse trusts us and will move away from pressure. We can now safely ask him to pick up his feet for us.

Start with the left front leg. Begin by petting down that leg all the way to his hoof to double check that he's completely comfortable with your hands touching his leg, hoof, etc. Now apply just a little pressure with your hand at the top of his leg (where it attaches to the body) until he shifts his weight just slightly away from your push. When he does, reward him with a release of the pressure and verbal praise to let him know he did what you wanted. When he'll take weight off the foot you want to pick up every time you ask, then you are ready to pick up that foot. Do this procedure to his right front leg as well.

When picking up the left front foot begin by pressing on the top of his left leg at the shoulder until he shifts his weight off his foot. Now, place your hand in between his front legs and hold that leg just above the back of the knee. Try to lift it up, but only about a half inch or so. In effect, you are just bending a weightless leg at the knee joint, which will cause the foot to leave the ground. As the foot comes off the ground, cup the hoof in your right hand (see photos opposite page) and let it rest there for a few seconds before returning it gently to the

BOB SAYS:
Don't grab the hoof or the horse will feel trapped. Just cup it gently in your hand.

ground. Repeat many times, praising him each time. Now put a cue (signal for him to pick up the left foot) on it, by either applying a voice command such as "Pick Up!" or just tapping above the inside of the knee with your left hand until he picks up that foot. When he does, cup the foot with your right hand. When he understands this, transfer the foot to your left hand so you can work on it with your right hand. If you're left handed, you won't have to perform this last step. Don't grab the foot, just cup it, and he won't fear being trapped. Repeat the procedure on the right front foot.

Pick up the back feet using a similar approach. When picking up the left hind, step in close to the horse by his flank area and apply pressure with your right hand on his hindquarters at the top of his leg until he shifts

BOB SAYS:
If he snatches his hoof away, you have moved through the steps too quickly.

These series of photos (above and next page) shows how to start to pick up his hind foot.

BOB SAYS:
Safety first when working on the back legs of any horse. Make sure you have completed all the sections prior to this one.

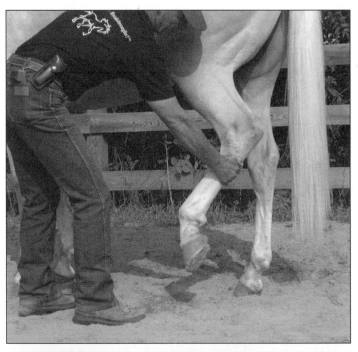

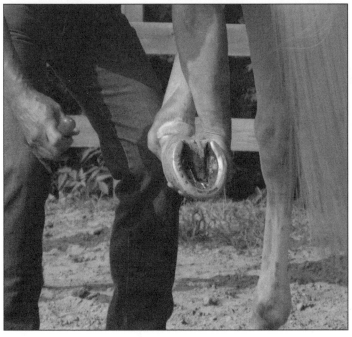

his weight. Then slip that same hand down to just below his hock and lift the foot gently off the ground. When he'll pick it up every time you ask, put your cue on it (saying "Pick Up!" or tapping with your hand just below the hock). When he lifts his foot, cup it in your left hand; you can then begin to clean or pick the hoof with your other hand. When you're done, place it back on the ground, don't just drop it. Remember to release it gently. Reverse the directions and repeat on the other side. ❧

Bob on Teaching Horses

It doesn't really matter how old your horses are; they can all learn new things. Young horses will need a little bit more repetition, and older horses may get annoyed if you overdo things. One thing that's important to recognize is that horses learn on a level equivalent to kindergarten or first grade, if you are comparing them to children.

What I mean by that is, whether the horse is 15 years old or 2 years old, they learn the way that a 5- or 6-year-old child would learn. They need a lot of repetition. And, in the beginning, they need a lot of praise when they get something right. They also will not learn from fear. Yelling, screaming or hitting have no place here. Just imagine if you asked a child what 2 plus 2 was, he answered, "Three!" and you smacked him across the face and

said, "Get it right next time, stupid!" Well, you'd be doing a whole lot more harm. You would not be creating an environment that was conducive to learning.

I don't think anybody reading this book would actually do that to a child, but sometimes people do that to horses because we simply don't look at them as 5- or 6-year-old children; we look at them as these large animals that somehow should know what it is we want — magically! I think it's very unfair to ask a horse to do anything that we haven't taught him to do on cue.

Horses can do everything we ask them to do, but we have to teach them the cues and signals for getting it right. They need lots of repetition and praise in the beginning. Force and intimidation just don't work.

V.S.S. Lesson

THIS LESSON SHOWS OUR HORSE HOW TO BE MINDFUL, BUT MOST OF ALL, SAFE TO BE AROUND

V.S.S. stands for **Very Special Safety** lesson. This is where our horse becomes a good citizen. He'll learn to pay attention to us, not to push into or over us, to move out of our way, and become respectful. We'll start him going forward and lungeing. It'll also reinforce what we learned on page 46, not to pull back when tied.

> **BOB SAYS:**
> This is one of my most important lessons. This will make your horse a good, solid citizen and a pleasure to be around.

Start by draping a lead rope over the horse's head just behind his ears so the ends hang down on each side of his face. Hold each end and apply about 2-3 pounds of pressure by pulling downward. Undo the pressure with *absolutely any* downward movement of his head. If his head goes up, which is natural and to be expected, don't add more pressure, just maintain the 2-3 pounds until it moves downward.

Left: Here is the starting position with the lead rope draped over the horse's head. In the second photo at right, the horse has yielded to the pressure of the rope on his poll and lowered his head.

53

Practice this movement every day for a few months. Your horse will get better and better, and eventually you will have altered his natural response of raising his head against the pressure and conditioned him to drop it, thereby relieving the pressure. When you can pull down hard on the rope and his head drops, you can rest assured he won't pull back when tied or panic if he steps through a rein or gets tangled with the lead rope.

The next step is to teach him to move forward. Start by holding the lead rope right at the snap by the halter with your

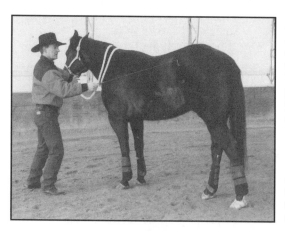

Left: Teach him to move forward by tapping his hip with the whip. The lighter the pressure, the lighter your horse will be as the final result.

Below: Notice, now I've turned my shoulders to walk with him.

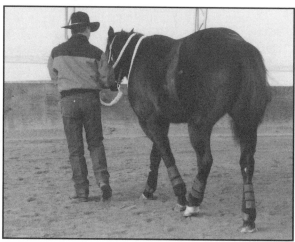

left hand and while pushing forward (pushing your horse towards the left) with that hand, use a dressage whip in your right hand to lightly tap the point of his right hip (you're giving his hip a cue or, as I say it, "Cue his hip") until he moves forward. When he does walk, stop tapping and stop pushing; just turn to face the direction he's going, change the lead into your right hand (put slack in the lead rope) and walk along with him for about 5 or 10 steps. Then stop him and reward with a good pet. Repeat the procedure over and over again. As he starts to understand what you're asking, you can start taking your left hand further and further away from the snap, while still pointing with your hand in the direction of travel.

> **BOB SAYS:** Eventually, your horse will be so light that all you have to do is direct your eyes at his hip and he moves!

> **BOB SAYS:** Don't lunge your horse in mindless and never-ending circles. Two or three circles in each direction are plenty and will give you a clear insight as to his mood.

You can also get rid of the whip and just twirl the other end of the lead rope at the hip. Ask your horse to walk forward while you walk with him but start gradually moving further and further back along his body until he's walking forward and you're walking off to the side behind his hip. In effect, you'll be pushing him with your energy rather than trying to pull him with your muscles.

Now begin to ask him to move around you in a circle. Show him the direction with your left hand on the lead rope (if he's too close to you, chase his nose away by twirling the tail end of the lead rope at his nose, being sure not to hit it accidentally) then drive the hindquarters and let him circle around you. Try not to keep driving him relentlessly; we want our horse to continue to move until we ask him to stop.

> **BOB SAYS:** The techniques used in this lesson not only make your horse easier to lead and tie but also give you an exercise which can regain his attention and focus if he becomes excited.

Let him circle around you only two or three times before asking him to stop. You'll do this by deliberately running your left hand down the lead rope about 2 feet or so toward the snap. At the same time, stare at his hip with your mean face while twirling the tail end of rope toward the hip, asking him to disengage the hindquarters and stop. Rub him enthusiastically, let him rest for a few seconds and repeat on the other side. Now let's try to keep him circling but start moving his circles around the arena. If your horse won't move away from you when you ask him to, focus on his shoulder and twirl the tail end of the rope at it; he should move sideways a few steps while continuing to circle. When he does, make sure you release the pressure. ❧

Left: I'm showing the horse that I'd like him to go. I'm pushing him forward with my left hand.

Above: Here he's moving in the direction that my left hand requested while I focus my eyes on driving the hip. Notice, I've also released the rope when he correctly went where I want.

Bob on How to Praise Your Horse

As far as praise, our horse's skin is far more sensitive than ours. I've been told that their skin is up to five, six, or even seven times more sensitive than human skin. So if you would like your girlfriend, boyfriend, husband or wife to come home from work and just slap you on the back as hard as they could five or six times and say, "Hi, Honey! I really like you!" then you go ahead and do that to your horse.

But if you'd rather they came home and they gave you a good rub on your back, then maybe that's what you should do for your horse. My rule of thumb — it's kind of simple — if you can hear the pat, it's probably too hard. So think about rubbing your horse or petting your horse rather than slapping him.

Now, as far as praise goes, I do believe that if you're enthusiastic with your horse in the beginning, then he will be more willing to try for you down the road. He likes knowing when he got it right.

It's more important, however, to release the pressure you were using to get the action you requested. This will eventually be his real source of knowing he got it right. But in the beginning, the additional use of praise added to that release of pressure goes a long way towards your horse figuring out your request.

Now, once a horse has learned something and knows it, he doesn't need as much praise. Again, the release will be praise enough. In fact, too much praise actually becomes a distraction to the horse! If you're anything like me, when someone says, "Good job, Bob!" that's nice. I like it. But if they say, "Good job, Bob! I really appreciate it! I want to hug you..." I think, "Get away from me!" It's too much. Some horses are really affectionate, but most of them aren't. They like a little bit of praise, but lavish praise can be too much of a good thing. It can be distracting.

Bob on Knowing the Difference

We need to recognize when our horse is confused and doesn't understand what we're asking of him and when he simply does not want to do it. Now, usually you know when your kids don't want to go to school. They may say, "I don't feel good." But if they're bouncing on a trampoline and throwing a football to their friends, they're not sick, they just don't _want_ to go to school. And, you, as a parent, learn which is which.

You'll need to learn to tell when your horse is confused and doesn't understand and when he is looking for a way out. If he is confused, then you'll step back and figure out what you can do to make it easier to succeed, rather than push him to failure.

But if there's a time when your horse does understand your request but he says, "Well, I just don't want to do that today! Isn't Monday my day off?" and he decides not to do it and you let him decide not to do it, the following days won't get better. He'll have figured you out.

So you've got to recognize the difference between "I don't understand!" and "It's Monday, my day off!" The former you'll work with, the latter you won't accept. You say, "Sure you work! You're my partner, and we work on Mondays!"

Building Confidence

TEACH YOUR HORSE TO BE BRAVER!

In order to build our horse's confidence and also work on his emotions, we'll ask for a little speed while he circles around us at the end of our lead rope. Speed helps to raise the horse's emotional level and brings him just a little bit out of his comfort zone. When we work on getting him excited and then calming him down, he gets used to being able to calm down. He can better deal with new places, horses, or strange situations if he has this emotional training.

> **BOB SAYS:**
> Remember this series of small successes continues to build your horse's confidence. He'll feel good about himself and will want to try for you when you make another request.

A good trot will suffice. As you move with him around the arena place a few ground poles in his path and just let him trot over them.

Then lean a pole against the bottom rail of the fence of the arena to make a little jump. Ask him to jump over it. Raise the height level gradually until he'll take a 3-foot jump for you.

Then try something solid like a block or a barrel for him to jump. Ask him to trot over water or a tarp or a plastic bag. Use as many objects as you can think of, but use baby steps and lots of them to accomplish your feats.

> **BOB SAYS:**
> Use baby steps and lots of them to accomplish your feats!

Now stand about 10 feet away from a fence or wall of the arena and ask your horse to go through the space between you and the fence/wall. Keep at it, narrowing down the gap gradually until he'll pass between you and the fence when you're only 3 feet away.

Try to get him to walk between two objects (barrels, mounting block, etc.) placed only 3 feet apart. When he'll do all this without any trepidation, he should be easier to load in the trailer as most trailer stalls are about 40 inches wide and we've already taught him to go forward, to go between objects and to walk over tarps, etc.

This whole section is designed to build confidence in your horse, so take your time and have some fun with it! When you can do everything mentioned here, you might wish to use a longer line (a lunge line or 20-30 foot lariat) and ask him to do all the above while further away from you. ❧

Above: Suzanne walks Lukka over a tarp. Below: Lukka jumps a small jump. Play with your horse: these are all fun exercises and you and your horse will benefit!

Remember, take baby steps to reach a goal. Figure out your final goal and break it down to many baby steps. Don't start with the goal.

Bob on Building Confidence and Becoming Partners

I'd like to tell you a little story about a horse I bought. His name is Blackjac (he is the black horse on the cover and in many of the pictures within this book). This horse was being ridden in a clinic, and, to make a long story short, the horse and owner weren't a good match; she couldn't get him to do anything. She asked me to jump on during one of the breaks. I knew immediately that this horse had a lot of talent, but he had some issues.

The woman called me a couple of weeks later, asking me if I want to buy him. Like I said, I thought this horse had a lot of talent, so I bought the horse. We stopped him from biting, and kicking, and let him just be a horse for a month or so. Then I started riding and training him. We got a pretty good reining spin on him, a nice stop, and had started on lead changes. I just thought, "Wow! I made a good decision. This is a great little horse!"

On another day, I had been working Blackjac for about 45 minutes. My partner, Suzanne, asked me to join her and her Icelandic, Lukka, on a trail ride.

Well, Blackjac had never been outside a ring before but I didn't know that. He spooked 10 times just up the driveway! We finally got him in the park, and I actually got him to lead the ride, to trot, (he did

a lot of spooky side-to-sides). He also spooked around every puddle of water, but I eventually got him to where he enjoyed being out there, and even got a little canter going.

Anyway, we went around a bend and he hit the breaks. I was almost up around his ears! He had spotted a deer, a little baby fawn. He started to tremble with all four legs splayed out. Blackjac was literally shaking in his boots. But the deer was looking at him and it was shaking, too! Watching these two grazing animals terrorizing each other was actually comical for a while, but as the deer finally started to run off, I encouraged Blackjac to chase it (in a safe-to-the-deer way). I said, "Go get him, Jack!" And he did — he went after him. I swear he started to puff up his chest, stick it out and look like he had just chased away that "nasty deer!" He was really proud of himself.

And that's what I mean about your horse's confidence coming from you. If I had gotten all 'clutchy,' kicked him when he stopped at the deer and had gotten afraid, I would have proved to him it was right to be afraid. Instead, I kind of laughed and encouraged him to go after the deer. My confidence helped to build his confidence.

Trailer Loading

MAKE TRAILER LOADING SAFER WITH THESE EXERCISES

We've done all our preparation and have some basic tools to work with so it's time to load our horse into the trailer.

BOB SAYS:
Butt bar lesson: Remove the butt bar from the trailer and in a round pen or small corral, apply pressure to his hind end with the butt bar until he moves forward away from the pressure.

Remember to make it easy for him to succeed, don't test him to failure. Before you get your horse, make sure the trailer is secured to the tow vehicle and that everything (buckets, rakes, tools, etc.) is removed from the stall area. Move the divider all the way over to one side, and open all the windows and doors so the trailer doesn't look like a dark cave (where a bear might be hiding). Teach him to move away from the pressure of a butt bar before loading him in the trailer.

Now, standing by his left side, take your horse with halter and lead rope toward the trailer. He'll probably stop somewhere about 5 to 10 feet in front of it. This is normal; let him stay here calmly to establish in his mind that he is safe at this distance from the trailer.

After a few moments, cue his hip with the tail end of the lead rope (or tap with a dressage whip if necessary) to ask him

BOB SAYS:
Remember the **Vowel Method** to cue his hip! Always start with an "ASK," and your horse will become that much more responsive.

Cue His Hip

Remember, the hip and the hindquarters are the engine of the horse. This is where all the movement starts. As you learned in the V.S.S. lesson on page 53, you can either twirl the end of the lead rope or tap his hip with the whip. As your horse becomes more responsive, you may simply be able to look at his hip to cue it and cluck.

63

In this series of photos, Suzanne has asked her horse to load into the trailer.

You'll notice we are using a step-up trailer, because a trailer with a ramp tends to elevate the horse's head. He's then more likely to bump his head on the trailer ceiling. In a step-up, he is more likely to look down at the trailer floor.

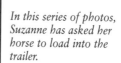

to move forward. Release your cue on any movement forward, even if it's just one step or even a slight shift forward, and let him rest. Repeat this sequence while gradually getting him closer and closer to the trailer in a relaxed and calm frame of mind. Eventually you'll have your horse at the back of the trailer.

Now, when you ask him again to move forward your horse may choose any of several options. He could lower his head to look down at the floor of the trailer or paw at it with one foot. Either is a good sign telling you he's thinking about going in. Release your pressure and reward this thought with a good rub and verbal praise. Ask again and eventually he'll put one foot in the trailer. When he does, undo your pressure, praise and ask him to back that foot off or out of the trailer.

After you load and unload this foot fifty times or so, ask for both front feet to go in. Load and unload both feet fifty times or so, releasing and praising each time. You're also teaching your horse to unload slowly and safely, which is a very good thing to teach.

Also, all this standing with both feet in the trailer will get his back legs tired so he'll be more inclined to finally go in fully when you ask him to. So ask; he'll put those two front feet in and when you ask for him to continue to move forward, he'll probably step all the way in.

When he does, let him rest there for several minutes before asking him to back out. This cements the idea (using the natural trait of laziness) that it's nice to stay in the trailer; no work here! While continuing to load and unload the horse, start gradually narrowing the space until the divider is in its normal position, start hooking up the butt bar, open and close windows and doors. Finally pack up fully and take your horse for a short ride (no more than a mile or so on the first ride) then back him out, praise him and give him some down time.

TRAILERING PROBLEMS SOLVED

I told you that when the horse arrives at the back end of the trailer he has options, and not all of them are good. So what can go wrong and how do you fix it? You'll need your dressage whip and all your wits about you to deal with some of these potentially very dangerous situations.

BOB SAYS:
Make sure you have gone through all the steps preceding this one before attempting to solve any severe trailering problems.

First, he could simply go backwards instead of forward. If he does, go with him and start tapping with a dressage whip on the point of his hip. Continue to tap, increasing both the speed and the intensity of the taps the further back he goes. As soon as he stops his feet, discontinue tapping, wait 10 seconds, then ask him to go forward again. Repeat as necessary.

Second, he could try to run away to the right, away from you. Since you've already taught him to follow the feel of the rope, he should stop when all the slack is removed from the lead rope. Redirect his nose into the trailer and ask for forward motion once again.

Third, he could rear up. While holding the end of the lead rope and watching your horse closely, apply swift taps with your whip to his front legs below the knee until he starts to come down. Again, ask for forward motion and repeat as necessary.

Fourth, he could choose to escape by going left, through or over you. Move aside quickly and again strike the horse below the knee with the whip until he stops going in this direction. If your horse prefers this evasion option, you might choose to remain about 10 feet behind your horse and use a longer (15-20 foot) lead rope. Send him forward and if he attempts to scoot out to the left of the trailer, don't try to stop him, but drive him faster by twirling your lead rope "tail." Direct him on about a 20-25 foot diameter circle (your horse will be about 10-12 feet away from you) until his nose once again points toward the trailer. Stop twirling as he approaches the back of the trailer. If he shows any interest in the trailer, reward this by taking him 20 feet away from the back of the trailer and pet him for a few moments in this non-threatening spot, all the while facing the trailer (remem-

BOB SAYS:
Uncertain of your horsemanship skills, ask your trainer to help here.

66

ber the "approach and retreat" method, pages 29-30). Then repeat. Whenever he shows more interest in the trailer, take him away and reward him. If he once again tries to run away to the left (his choice), just send him faster on the circle until he's facing toward the trailer. After a half hour or hour of this, he'll probably figure out what you want.

Your horse has no right to ever hurt you intentionally and rearing up or trying to run you over could do just that. Even though we love our horses, we cannot allow this type of aggressive behavior as it shows a lack of respect and is extremely dangerous to us. However, if you go through all the steps prior to this trailer loading section, your horse will most likely not demonstrate these negative reactions. ໕

Bob on the Big, Bad Trailer

We recently had a horse come to one of our Horsemanship Breakthrough Weeks. It is a week long clinic and seminar and a lot of fun for all.

For this particular clinic, everyone was supposed to be at the ranch Sunday afternoon. One participant had called late Sunday night. She had just spent 4 hours trying unsuccessfully to load her horse and was going to try again Monday morning. We got another call that after 3 hours of trying, they were on their way.

Well, she had a great time and did a lot of things that we've discussed in this book, two of which were the "Go Forward" cue (see pages 53-56), and asking her horse to back up off the lead rope. She developed a great bond with her horse but she was still anxious about whether her horse would get back in the trailer.

Now, Suzanne and I usually spend about 30 minutes of private time with each of our students that week on whatever they want. Obviously, it was this woman's request that we teach her horse to load into the trailer.

I worked with the horse, and not only did I get her in the trailer, but I taught her to load in just 28 minutes. Someone was timing it. We had this horse loading herself. We would just point her at the trailer and she would go in calmly and stay in. And, when we asked her to back out, she would come out easily. This is a lesson that will stay with the horse for the rest of her life.

It's not about getting the horse to go in the trailer, it's about teaching her to go forward and back on request. If that leads to loading into and out of the trailer calmly and safely, then that is great. We had worked on the basics all week, the baby steps, and then the final goal, which was loading, was easy.

Above: While we can't very well teach a horse not to be afraid, we can teach him what to do when he does become afraid. At first, stop his feet and look at the object that's scaring him. Eventually, he should just ignore scary things because he trusts you. Above: This is what the finished horse should look like in this situation. (Incidentally, this is Blackjac, described in Bob on Building Confidence and Becoming Partners on page 62.)

Spook Proofing
HOW TO TEACH HIM TO MANAGE HIS FEAR

Now that he trusts us and has some confidence in himself, it's time to alter that natural spook, bolt, and "get out of Dodge" reaction to one of stopping his feet and looking at what's scaring him.

Begin with your horse in his halter and a 30-foot rope attached to it. Stand 10 feet or so in front of your horse. While facing him and holding the other end of the rope in your hand, just say "Boo"! Don't say it with too much vigor, just enough to have him hear it, but hopefully not move away. If he stands still, go up and pet him. Now go back to your original starting point and try again with just a bit more energy.

Above: Suzanne says "BOO!" to Lukka.

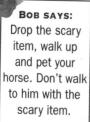

Keep repeating, and each time he stands, go up and pet him. Build up your "boos" until you can shout them at him and he'll do no more than raise his head up.

At this point you should add "poofing" sounds, then "raspberry" sounds. Then make these sounds while "airplaning" your arms.

Each time he stands still, quit trying to scare him. Walk up with a happy face and pet him. Try shaking an old empty feed bag or garbage bag at him, then go to waving a tarp. If he doesn't move, drop the object, walk up to him slowly and pet your horse. Remember your objective is to scare him a little *but not too much!*

Left: Build up from poofing and raspberry sounds to a feed bag or a garbage bag. If he doesn't move, drop the object and walk up to him slowly and pet him.

Right: Remember your objective is to scare him a little but not too much!

Above: Work up to scarier things, such as throwing a tarp in the air.
Above, Lukka stands for Suzanne while she throws a tarp way up!
Remember, baby steps to work up to this final goal.

Your horse is learning that if he simply stops his feet and looks at what is scaring him, the scaring stops. However, if he does try at any point during the lesson to run off, go with him while you continue scaring him with whatever you're currently using but lower your intensity dramatically (also don't get behind him — he'll think the scary object is chasing him). Try to stay out in front laterally (in front of the horse's withers, not directly in his path) where he can see you; use the rope and gently tug at it to encourage him to look at you and stop his feet. When he does, you immediately quit scaring him, drop the object, and go pet him.

> **BOB SAYS:**
> Take your time with this lesson. It doesn't have to be done in one day. End with a small success and begin again the next day.

This is not a sacking out or desensitizing lesson. We are not trying to get the horse used to the bags, sounds or tarps; we're trying to teach him to handle his fear. Desensitizing certainly does work, but only with those objects used. The spook-proofing teaches him to stop his feet and look at what is scaring him, no matter what it is *(that's why we don't approach the horse with the scary object; we drop it and walk up to pet him without it).* 🐾

> **BOB SAYS:**
> Again, evaluate your horsemanship skills and get the aid of a trainer when you need it!

Bob on Handling Fear

Suzanne and I had purchased a horse from a nice fellow whom we've bought horses from before. We went over and rode three or four horses but we both really liked the look in this one horse's eye, and decided to buy him. Our thought was to put some training on him and eventually resell him. We didn't know exactly what kind of training he'd had but he could walk, trot and canter. However, he was spooky and really afraid of abrupt movements near him and walking over unfamiliar objects, even ground poles.

We purchased the horse (Ace) and decided to take him to the Equine Event East in Virginia with us. We were demonstrating our techniques in many different exhibitions at this expo.

In one of our presentations, we showed how to teach a horse to handle his fear, through spook proofing. We used Ace as it was obvious he had never learned any spook training. He did a great job.

He was standing quietly while I frantically waved bags at him, opened and closed umbrellas.

We then invited the expo audience to come down and try to scare him with me in the saddle. Suzanne was admitting people, one at a time, to wave a plastic bag or whatever they had on hand. None of them could get this horse to spook. He was very calm and was looking at me as if to say, "Should we run?" and I would say, "No." He just stood there calmly while the crowd did their best to frighten Ace.

So then Suzanne decided to let five people in all at once! Each with a different object! We had a tarp, an umbrella, a jacket, someone waving a stick with a plastic bag at the end, and even a lunge whip snapping. Ace took it bravely. In fact, so well I decided to ride in amongst them all. We kind of snaked through the crowd and he did so well, I decided to ride him right over the tarp on the ground. In about 10 minutes, he was walking back and forth over the tarp.

By the end of the demo, Suzanne decided that Ace was not for sale anymore! She was going to keep him.

So once again, you can't teach a horse not to be afraid, but you can teach him how to handle his fear.

Saddling

PROPER SADDLING TECHNIQUES CAN SET THE TONE FOR YOUR WHOLE RIDE

Now we should be ready to saddle up. You've approached your horse many times already with the rope and the blanket so he should accept your approaching with the saddle.

> **BOB SAYS:**
> Even seasoned veterans can benefit from this saddling exercise.

Let him see it coming, but don't approach like you're carrying nitro-glycerin; walk up with your happy face, carrying that saddle out front. Let him sniff it and then place it gently on his back. Make sure the stirrups, latigo, cinch straps, etc., don't hit his sides. (You do not want to hit the horse with any of these straps. Secure them out of the way while saddling.) You should also be able to place the saddle on his back from either side, so practice both ways.

Now take the girth strap and apply just a bit of pressure to your horse's cinch area. When he accepts it, go ahead and tighten the cinch up. Don't pull too tightly, just enough so that when he moves the saddle will stay put.

Ask him to circle around you once or twice before retight-

Left: Let the horse look at the saddle and sniff it if he wants to. Above: Place it on his back gently. Don't bump him with the stirrups.

ening the cinch. This intermediate step allows your horse to relax and exhale during the saddling because he trusts that you won't pinch him or tighten so much that he can hardly breathe.

SADDLING THE GROUCHY VETERAN

If you do have a grouchy horse who gets anxious or pins his ears as you start to cinch up, your first step is to make sure the saddle fits. Saddle fit is the number one reason most horses object to the saddling and mounting procedures. Think about going to class in a pair of jeans that are two sizes too small or with a pebble in your shoe. How much of your attention would be on your teacher? If you do need help checking this, seek out someone who is knowledgeable on saddle fitting.

If your saddle does fit, however, and he still gets cranky we'll have to take a small step backwards and fix this obvious "hole" in his training. Remove the saddle and use your arm to put pressure (just a little) in the cinch area. Pet the horse each time he allows you to do this without out getting upset or pinning his ears. Then, proceed to use a towel or saddle blanket. Drape it over the horse's back and reach under his belly and pull it up gently like it was a cinch. Again, pet him whenever he accepts.

If he does get upset, use lighter pressure and build up gradually. Now try the saddle again. Tighten the cinch gradually and in stages.

Let the Air Out!

Horses will expand themselves (or hold their breath) when we tighten the cinch. This is a natural reaction on their part. Having him circle around causes him to breathe and you can tighten the cinch a little more in several small steps.

Some people will knee the horse in the belly to force him to exhale but as you can imagine, this method is not particularly appreciated by the horse and he will, eventually, become that grouchy veteran.

Left: Fix the "hole" in his training! Use your arm to put pressure (just a little) in the cinch area. Pet him if he allows this without getting upset or pinning his ears.

Below: Then proceed to use a towel or saddle blanket draped under his belly. Again, pet him if he allows this.

1. Tighten just so the saddle won't fall off. 2. Send the horse circling around you once or twice to the left and tighten the cinch a little more. 3. Send the horse around to the right once or twice and tighten once again. Once your horse realizes that the saddle won't

hurt and that you won't pinch or tighten too hard or too fast, the problem should disappear. It may take several sessions and this is a good method to do every time you saddle. 🐾

Bob on Saddle Fitting

At a clinic, one of my clients was bucked off immediately after mounting. The client told me that this was the behavior problem he was attending the clinic to solve. When I finally caught his horse, I noticed that the pommel was jabbing the horse's withers.

Another client complained that her horse wouldn't stand still for mounting. After seeing how the saddle was poking and pinching him, I fully understood why.

A third client had rescued a horse. The horse was thin when she first bought him and completely manageable to ride. As he gained weight, he became more difficult to ride, often bucking her off. We realized the sole problem was the saddle fit. As the horse gained condition and weight, the old saddle, made to fit him when he was thin, did not fit anymore.

We changed saddles on all these horses and the bad behavior immediately went away. Their behavior problems were due only to incorrectly fitted saddles!

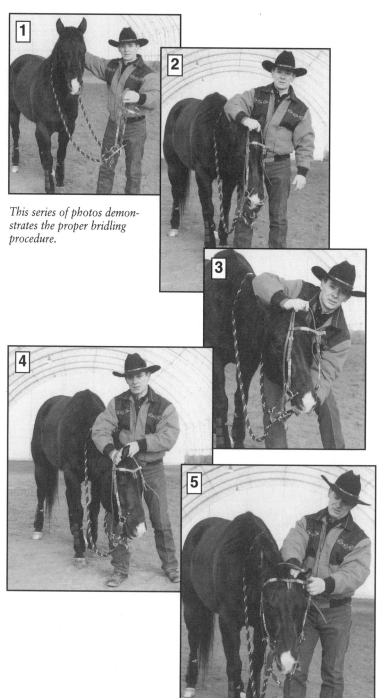

This series of photos demonstrates the proper bridling procedure.

Bridling

ALL RIDERS WILL APPRECIATE THIS NO-HASSLE WAY TO BRIDLE YOUR HORSE

Remember when we first started working to gain our horse's trust? We asked him to drop his head and we rubbed his nose and gums gently. We were able to put our fingers in the side of his mouth, which caused him to open his mouth.

Lets do this "open your mouth" exercise again, but now we'll add a step of cupping the horse's ears, one at a time, and bending them forward.

When the horse will lower his head, bring it to the side, open his mouth and let you touch his ears, you will have basically already taught all the steps involved in bridling. Putting the actual bridle and bit in place should now be a piece of cake.

Firstly, put the reins over the horse's head so you'll have something to hold onto should he decide to walk off. Then, hold the bridle at its top with your right hand while you are standing at your horse's left. Now, place this hand between the horse's ears, letting the bit hang down just below his mouth.

With your left hand, ask the horse to open his mouth (using a finger or two in the corner) and when he does, raise your right hand upward until the bit enters his mouth.

You may not have to touch the bit with your left hand at all, but it's all right to do so if you need to guide (not push) it into the horse's mouth.

Now grip the top of the bridle with your left hand which will free up your right hand to

> **BOB SAYS:**
> If your horse is resistant to bridling, make sure his teeth are floated and his ears are free of sores and ear mites.

> **BOB SAYS:**
> If you can't cup your horse's ears or bend them forward (and there are no health issues), go back to page 31.

77

cup the horse's right ear and push it forward under the crown piece of the bridle. Then repeat with the left ear. Buckle your throat latch and you're ready to mount. Be careful not to bump the horse's teeth with the bit. If you're using a nose band, it should be snug but not tight.

To remove the bridle after your ride, just reverse the process. After opening the throat latch, lift the crown piece over the left ear, then the right ear, and let the horse drop the bit out of his mouth (don't pull it out).

When you go through this bridling procedure, I can almost guarantee that your horse will take the bridle every time you ask him, provided there is nothing physically wrong and he hasn't had a previous bad experience. Ultimately, every time you ask him to, your horse will drop his head, reach down, open his mouth and practically take the bridle himself. ❧

Are Boo Boos the Bridling Problem?

If after you progress through these bridling and sacking out exercises and you still have a problem handling your horse's ears or mouth, you may have another situation. If you cup your horse's ear and he pulls his head up with a sudden stricken look in his eye or if there's constant fussing with the bit or his mouth, then it's time for a health check from your vet.

Your horse may have a sore or a bug infestation in his ear. Or his teeth may need special attention. (Horses need their teeth checked and/or floated twice a year.)

Also, be alert to signs of impending problems. If your horse, a consistent good horse to bridle, suddenly becomes bad, possibly it is the start of an ailment requiring your vet. Get it checked before it gets worse!

Taming the Clipper Monster

HOW TO CLIP YOUR HORSE WITHOUT TWITCHES, EAR TWISTING OR SEDATION

Now that our horse is taking the bridle nicely, we can also teach him to accept clippers. It's important that we focus on the "teaching" and "accepting" part of the previous sentence.

> **BOB SAYS:** Always begin with a lesson plan so you can work smarter, not harder.

We are, by definition, eliminating the use of twitches, ear twisting or even sedation as a means to accomplish our task. We will therefore define our goal as teaching our horse to accept clipping anywhere on his head calmly and comfortably. We must now develop a lesson plan, breaking down the steps to our goal into logical, manageable bits. Then we'll implement it gradually. In this way, we will build our horse's confidence in stages, helping him to succeed, rather than testing him to failure.

So, let's start at our desk, or the kitchen table, making a list of lots of things to rub on our horse's head. These items will familiarize him with both physical contact and noise (remember, clippers buzz!). A sample list might consist of the following items:

1. Your hand
2. Sponge
3. Washcloth
4. Towel
5. Candy wrapper
6. Aluminum foil
7. Crumpled newspaper
8. Plastic bag
9. Brush
10. Clipper

There are obviously hundreds of different objects you could use, but most horses require only 5-15 items in order to learn the lesson properly.

Left: Here I am using item #3, a wash cloth, from the list on page 79. I'll also add buzzing sounds as I rub around and inside the ear with my hand.

Right: Here the horse is accepting the clippers calmly. I'll make this first session short. Just one small section and then I'm done.

After you compile your list, rearrange it numerically starting with what you think would be the easiest for your horse to tolerate and ending with what would be the most difficult for him. The first item on your list must be your hands and the last item should be the clippers.

Begin by rubbing your hand all over your horse's head. He must be comfortable with you rubbing his nose, his ears, his gums, etc. If you encounter resistance to being touched in a certain spot, use the **approach and retreat method** (see pages 29-30) until the resistance is eliminated.

When your horse is completely comfortable with your hand anywhere around his head, in his mouth, nose and ears, then we can try item number two on our list, then item number three, etc. until the first nine items on your list have been used and your horse doesn't mind any of them.

The next step is item number ten, to use the actual clippers on your horse but without turning it on and without the blades. Rub him all over his head with the clippers, then try turning on the clippers (still without blades) and desensitize him to the feel of the vibration and sound. When he's very comfortable with this, you'll be ready to insert the blade, turn on your clippers and give him his first haircut.

Remember to make his first clipping session a relatively short one. Just do one small section and when you're done, give him a treat as a reward for being so very brave. We must always let him know when he does something right. ❧

Feeding Treats

I never use treats in an attempt to "bribe" a horse. I will, on occasion, give my horses a treat for doing something really brave but I do so sparingly. I do not want my horses to expect a treat and I never want them actively looking for one.

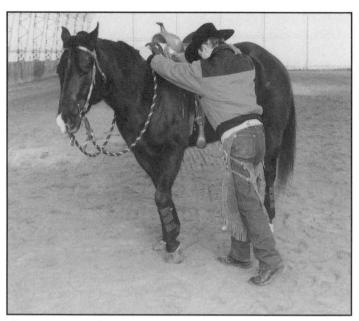

Both photos: Give the saddle a little push/pull so he knows what's coming and can balance himself. Here I am rocking Blackjac back and forth.

Mounting

THIS IS A GREAT EXERCISE FOR THE GREEN HORSE AS WELL AS TEACHING THE OLDER TO HORSE TO STAND

Whether we're mounting for the first time or trying to correct a horse that has developed the habit of moving off when we attempt to mount, the procedure is the same.

I have found that we need to announce our intentions to our horse. Give that saddle a little push/pull so he knows what's coming and can balance himself. Then stand by his shoulder away from the kicking end, and grip the mane and the rein with your left hand (if mounting from the left) and lightly put your left foot in the stirrup while looking at your horse's head (making sure he stays calm and relaxed).

Should the horse move, stay with him if you're able to by bouncing along on your right foot until he stops. When he stops, remove your foot from the stirrup. If he doesn't move

Above: I've just put a little weight in the stirrup.

Troubleshooting

If you can't stop your horse from moving when you are mounting with the steps mentioned in this chapter, disengage his hindquarters every time he takes a step or moves off (pages 44-46). This increased work load, in time, will convince your horse that it would be easier to just stand still.

83

when you place your foot in the stirrup, remove your foot and pet your horse! Do this three or four times from each side.

When you think he's comfortable, reassume the mounting position (rein and mane in left hand, right hand on the cantle while looking at his head), bounce on your right foot, and go up quickly. Land softly in the saddle, breathe, settle in and pet him for standing still and allowing you to mount. Always wait these

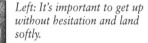

BOB SAYS:
Mount your horse from both sides! You never know when that will come in handy!

few seconds before asking him to move. That way he won't anticipate moving before you request it.

Once he has learned this lesson, you can simply approach the horse, push/pull the saddle, grip rein and mane, mount, land softly and relax.

If you are physically incapable of mounting from the ground in this manner, use a mounting block for assistance. Again, you should practice saddling and mounting from both sides. This not only prevents your horse from becoming one-sided, but allows you to mount safely, even on severely sloped terrain. ❧

Left: It's important to get up without hesitation and land softly.

Below: Remain relaxed and calm. Tell your horse he has done a good job standing still.

84

Bob on Saddling from the Horse's Point of View

I'd like to tell you a little story about saddling from the horse's point of view. If you've taught a horse to stand still while you mount, you have a responsibility to mount him safely and swiftly without causing him stress and, certainly, without causing him undue pain.

Well, I was at a clinic once where a particular woman took about four years to mount her horse. From the time she put her foot in the stirrup until the time she landed (and did she ever CLUNK down in that saddle), the poor horse was making all kinds of faces and begging for mercy. While she tugged and dragged herself up onto the horse, I went over and put my shoulder into her behind and heaved her up just that bit faster. The look of relief on that horse's face was worth any possible sexual harassment suit I might have gotten due to my impropriety.

We do spend time teaching our horse to stand still while we mount.

That becomes his job; our job is to be fit enough to get up on the horse. Put your foot in the stirrup, bounce once or twice, go up and over and land SOFTLY — that's what your horse is looking for.

If you are physically incapable of doing that, then take the time to teach your horse to stand next to a mounting block and use it! Walk up to the block, put your foot in the stirrup, up and over and land softly.

Do not pull on the saddle. The pressure you're exerting if you pull yourself up slowly puts enormous pressure on his withers, chest, spine, his whole back.

You also need to be absolutely sure of your saddle fit, even if you mount correctly. If the saddle is too tight, you'll pinch his withers, or if the saddle is too wide, then the pommel is actually sitting right on the withers. If you're not sure of fit, ask a knowledgeable saddle fitter to help you.

Bob (Once More) on Saddle Fit

Here is another example of just how truly important saddle fit is. A woman told me that her horse had been bucking since she bought it. The people she bought the horse from never told her about this problem. I asked her, "How long have you had him?" and she replied, "Five years and he has been bucking ever since I bought him."

I figured by this time she had learn to ride through his bucks, so I let her get on. I noticed that as soon as she landed in the saddle, it

seemed to fall apart. We asked her to step down in order to check it and sure enough, the saddle was sitting directly on the horse's withers! We discovered the saddle tree was broken and it was actually sitting directly on the horse's spine.

We switched saddles and the remainder of the clinic went fine. Here was a problem that someone was trying to fix with training when it was really an equipment problem.

Left: Suzanne has just asked her horse to move.

Below: She has engaged her seat bones, is looking out ahead and just squeezing with her inner calf.

The "Move" Cue

THIS IS PROBABLY THE MOST IMPORTANT CUE TO TEACH YOUR HORSE

As we know, a cue is simply a signal to the horse to do something. The "Move Cue" is really a signal for the horse to increase his leg speed — from stand to walk, from walk to trot, trot to canter, etc. This exercise is taught when the need arises no matter what the training level of the horse. Some horses will need to learn the "Move Cue" early on while others need it later, perhaps when they refuse to move in the arena, through water, mud or over a log on the trail.

> **BOB SAYS:**
> Without movement, there is no learning!

Many of you may know horses that have what you might consider too much movement. Horses that, in some cases, start moving even before we finish mounting. If this sounds familiar, start working through the ten parts of the following section (Phase 2: Advanced Exercises Under Saddle, page 91) in the sequential manner in which they are presented. What you will probably find out is that at some point during the sequence of lessons, your horse will stop moving. Then you will find out if your horse has a solid "Move Cue" to move or not!

If your horse does not respond to this cue consistently, you need to break from the sequence to teach the "Move Cue" and then return to Phase 2. In other words, if your horse doesn't move on request, you must correct this problem before you can teach anything else.

> **BOB SAYS:**
> Teach the "Move Cue" as soon as you need it. This cue supercedes everything else.

In order to show him that when we shift our seat and squeeze with our legs he should move forward every time, we'll start by bumping slowly and gently with both legs until he does move forward. At this point, one step, or even leaning forward, will do.

87

Also, do not use spurs to teach this lesson. Most horses working in an arena long enough may eventually need the occasional use of spurs (you must learn to use them correctly) but this lesson needs to be learned without them or their effectiveness will be compromised for the future.

Remember, the horse doesn't know what we are asking for, so he may look at us, shake his head, go sideways, etc. It is imperative for us to stay focused and concentrate on what is happening and continue bumping with our legs so we do not miss any form of forward movement.

You can increase intensity and/or speed if you feel this will help, but once you increase speed or intensity you cannot slow down or lighten the bumps. If you quit before the horse moves forward, you will have inadvertently taught him that if he waits long enough, the bumping will stop. So you need to start bumping with a speed and intensity that you can keep doing for what might turn out to be quite a while.

The first time he moves forward, immediately stop bumping with your legs (this is his reward for getting it right). His first move might be a step or two. That is fine! Praise him for doing the right thing and start the exercise again. Pretty soon your horse will figure out that the bumping is a request for forward movement and he will start responding by giving you impulsion on a lighter cue until eventually a slight squeeze will suffice.

Once your horse has definitely learned the "Move Cue" and knows that a squeeze of the legs means "move," you may use spurs or tap him with a dressage whip to offer additional encouragement should he not move when you ask him to. Once the horse moves, again, quit the use of all aides. Do not keep tapping with your legs or whip while he is moving or he will learn to always need that support from you.

However, he should continue to move until we ask him to

do something else. If he does quit moving before you ask him to, he'll need to be immediately corrected with leg pressure, whip or a slap with the tail end of the rein. Do not let him train you to consistently nag him with squeezes, bumps, or kicks every step or two.

I can tell you from experience that this is one of the most physically demanding lessons to teach a horse. As a matter of fact, when I ask one of my clinic assistants to work on a horse that doesn't have a "Move Cue," I usually get groans as a response. The reason for this is that it may take 300 bumps before a horse chooses to move forward and you cannot stop bumping until he does.

BOB SAYS:
There is no such thing as a dead-sided horse! If horses can feel a fly landing on them, they certainly can feel any slight change of pressure from your leg. Our job is to make our horses light and responsive to our "ASK."

BOB SAYS:
Help your horse with forward momentum, look out (not down,that will hinder his movement), put on your happy face, raise your energy level and GO FORWARD!

Once our horse understands this "Move Cue," we as riders do need to help our horse succeed. In addition to the bumping or a squeeze of the calf, we need to get our energy level up if we want our horse's energy level high too. Put on your happy face and look forward, not down at your horse (he will feel your head position and it will hinder his impulsion) and squeeze lightly with both calves simultaneously. You must be "riding" the horse, not just along for the ride. ❧

Tapping into V.S.S. (page 53)

If you have taught your horse to move forward from the ground during the V.S.S. lesson, you can use your dressage whip to help in this lesson. You would bump with your legs ten or fifteen times and then start tapping with the whip on his hip. Remember this step can only be used if your horse knows to move forward when you tap his hip.

Partnership Training
for Horse & Rider

PHASE 2

Advanced Exercises
Under Saddle

Above: Gaining control of the individual parts of the horse's body gives you the ability to deal with your horse in various situations, troubleshoot more quickly by determining where the problem actually is and evaluate new horses more quickly. Above: Bob and Suzanne performing at Equine Affaire in Ohio.

10 Parts to Partnership

GAINING CONTROL OF THE HORSE'S INDIVIDUAL BODY PARTS GIVES YOU CONTROL OVER HIS WHOLE BODY AS WELL AS HIS MIND

Your horse is a combination of body parts joined together to work in harmony. Gaining the control of these individual parts will make it easier for you to break down lessons into baby steps. This, in turn, will encourage your horse to learn and will provide him with many small successes along the way. Small successes will make him more confident and he will then become a more willing partner who wants to "try" for you.

> **BOB SAYS:**
> Small successes will make him feel good about himself and he will become a much more willing partner!

This gaining control of the parts is also a practical and efficient way of teaching and gives you the ability to deal with your horse in various situations. You will be able to troubleshoot more quickly by determining where the problem actually is and you will be able to evaluate new horses more quickly.

Throughout this book we need to work sequentially, but particularly in the following section. Because control of the jaw, Part 1, is necessary for us to gain control of the poll, Part

The 10 Parts to Partnership

Control all the parts below and your horse will become a true and willing partner!

1 JAW **2** POLL **3** EARS **4** NECK

5 FRONT FEET **6** WITHERS **7** BARREL

8 HINDQUARTERS **9** SHOULDER POINTS

10 NOSE

2 and so on. Be sure to work through the sequence in the order that follows. You'll soon be controlling and communicating effectively with your horse's entire body and mind. Maneuvers such as shoulder in, leg yields or reining spins can all be achieved easily through control of these individual parts.

BOB SAYS:
Make sure you've read the section on the "Move" cue before starting these lessons.

Proceed to the next part only when you've achieved solid results on the one with which you are currently working. You will not get the desired results if you jump from part to part. It will confuse your horse and considerably lengthen your training time. By the way, if you're having a problem with a certain part, the problem is most likely that you do not have the previous steps solid enough. In that case, go back to the previous step, work on it until the response is consistent, and then move on. Also, be sure to look for the riding tips I've included in this part of the book.

BOB SAYS:
Work through Parts 1 - 10 in consecutive order. Jumping out of sequence will just confuse your horse.

We're now ready to begin to gain control of various individual parts of the horse while mounted. But first I'd like to acquaint you with the equipment I personally use, explain why it is important and how it works.

RIDING EQUIPMENT

For our riding exercises, we'll use a snaffle bit with slobber straps and a continuous one-piece rope rein and a well-fitting saddle.

We use the snaffle because it is a mild bit that works by applying pressure on the corners of the horse's mouth. When used one side at a time, it provides a very clear signal to the horse without the use of pain.

Learning to move to the right when pressure is added from the

Above: Note the slobber straps and 8 - 10 foot reins.

94

rein to the bit will take a minimum of 500 repetitions on each side (and probably closer to 1,500) but once he's learned it, you'll be on your way to a true and rewarding partnership. This high number of repetitions is yet another reason for using a mild bit that will not create any discomfort for the horse. If you need to repeat an action thousands of times, how many times will your horse cooperate if he is in pain?

The movement from the weight of the slobber strap acts as a pre-cue when the horse starts to learn the lessons, allowing him to respond on less of a cue (we can start to ride on a loose rein if we choose to). This weight also provides instant relief of bit pressure when we release the rein.

I chose the rope rein because it's soft on our hands, but it also provides a firm hold if our horse pulls on us. It helps us to take the slack out of the rein slowly by making it easy to slide our hands from side to side, and it gives us the ability to release rein pressure quickly. You also need sufficient rein length of 8-10 feet in order to have at least 8 inches of slack on each side of the horse's neck. This exact length depends on the size of your horse.

BOB SAYS:
Here we go again with saddle fit, but it is very important. Check to make sure!

A saddle that fits your horse well is essential. As I discussed in an earlier chapter (see pages 74-75), if your saddle pinches the horse or causes any discomfort, it will be a constant distraction that will lengthen the learning process and make the experience unpleasant for your horse.

Your horse won't care which type of saddle you use, English or western. However, I do recommend a western saddle for the first ten rides or so on a young horse. A western saddle distributes the weight of the saddle and rider over a larger area of the horse's back. The saddle design gives you more security on the untrained horse which is more apt to make unexpected and sudden moves. Furthermore, the pommel on a western saddle will give you a better place to anchor your hand if your horse pulls on you when you request a "give," but more on that later!

Now, without further ado, on to gaining control of the individual parts and becoming a true partner with your horse. ❧

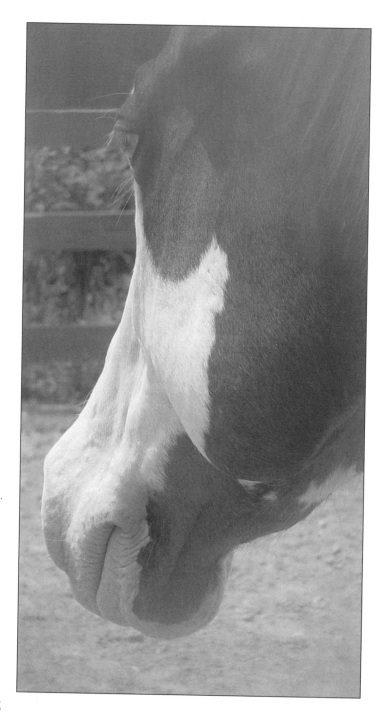

Part 1: The Jaw

THIS IS WHERE IT ALL BEGINS!

The jaw is the most important part to have control over. This is the key to all the other parts and is a huge step in convincing our horse that we are his best friend and leader.

> **BOB SAYS:**
> Control of the jaw is a huge step in truly becoming your horse's friend and partner.

In this jaw-control exercise, we'll learn to use our snaffle bit and the continuous rope rein, discussed in the previous chapter.

A significant point needs to be made here, and this applies to everything you teach your horse. Horses have two sides, left and right. Just because you teach something on one side (like mounting) it doesn't mean the horse knows it on the other. Why is this important? Let me give you an example.

A few years ago one of my friends injured his left knee. After he recovered from his injury he realized that he didn't have the strength he used to have in that knee and it was actually painful for him to try to mount his horse from the "normal" side.

The good news is that his horse was trained using my methods, so he was able to mount from the off-side with ease and his horse accepts it without problems.

This is not an assumption you can make safely on all horses, however. Many horses have not been trained to mount from the off-side and I have seen "trained horses" come totally unglued when someone tried to mount them from the wrong side! So it is essential that we teach everything on both sides of the horse. *Everything!*

We'll start on the right. Begin by taking the slack out of the right rein slowly until all the slack is out and there is a straight line from your right hand down the rein to the bit. If the horse pulls against you (the usual first reaction), it is impor-

Left: If your horse pulls against you, brace your hand against the pommel of the saddle. Hold this position until your horse's jaw moves in the direction of the rein you're using.

tant to brace your hand against the pommel of the saddle. This is not a tug of war you want him to win. If you're riding in an English saddle, locate a comfortable spot where you can best stabilize your hand.

BOB SAYS:
At the beginning of this lesson, any movement of the jaw in the correct direction must be rewarded with a release of the rein pressure.

Hold this position until your horse's jaw moves in the direction of the rein you're using, in this case the right. (Remember you are to hold, not pull, and under no circumstances are you going to jiggle the rein to "bump" the bit against your horse's mouth)

You need to know that what seems like a perfectly clear and easy task to you doesn't necessarily seem so to your horse. We assume that if we pick up the right rein, our horse should know that he should move his head to the right. If someone stuck their finger in the right corner of your mouth, you'd probably pull to the left or back or up to get that finger out of your mouth. Your horse will do the same until, by the process of elimination, he figures out that you will release your rein (i.e., take your finger out of his mouth) only when he moves his head to the right.

Now, *any* movement in the correct

BOB SAYS:
It is my firm belief that ninety percent of your safety on a horse depends on how well he will "give you his jaw" (my jargon for "give to the bit").

Right: Here the horse has "given" quite nicely!

direction counts, even a mere sixteenth of an inch! This movement of the jaw is called a "give." When the horse gives, we must immediately release the rein, providing him with instant relief from bit pressure. He is thereby rewarded for giving. When you first start the lesson, you may also hug or rub your horse enthusiastically. Eventually, the only reward he'll want is the release. In fact, too much praise actually becomes a distraction.

It's important to recognize when the horse gives. If the horse is pulling, he's not giving; if he has stopped pulling but has not moved his jaw, he's still not giving (this is the neutral position); hold until he "gives" in the correct direction. There must be energy in the give. Just wait, and resist the urge to pull him around but release the instant he "gives."

> **BOB SAYS:**
> Teaching even the seasoned veteran will make him a better and safer horse to ride. He will be listening to you more.

> **BOB SAYS:**
> Release the rein on any movement of the jaw toward the asking rein, even if it's a sixteenth of an inch. Even if you *think* the horse gave, RELEASE, because chances are he did.

We must develop the ability to pick up the reins slowly (this gives the horse a chance to respond with very little pressure on the bit) and release quickly when he gives. Remember, the object is to get the horse lighter, "giving" on a loose rein before all the slack is removed. We must concentrate on what we're doing, so that we can see the "give" and release immediately.

Left: Here the horse is walking and giving. See how soft and light he looks giving on a loose rein.

BOB SAYS:
Practice picking up your reins slowly in order to give your horse a chance to become lighter.

When we first teach this lesson, we should not be concerned with what his feet are doing. He could be walking, trotting, cantering or just standing still. We should also not be concerned with where he's going (so long as we feel safe, of course). Even if the horse is giving to the left, but walking to the right, it's okay at this point. We'll teach him to follow his nose (go where he's pointed) later.

You will eventually have to teach the horse to "give" on both sides at all his gaits. It is preferable to get 25-30 gives on one side before getting the same number (25-30) on the other side. Staying on one side for this number of repetitions tends to "soften" the neck faster. It's a good idea to count your "gives" to keep track of how many you have on each side.

BOB SAYS:
Your horse will start to understand when you've asked for about 350 gives, but he will really have learned the lesson at 1,500.

Usually your horse will start to understand what you're asking for around 350 gives (on each side) but he may go through several cycles of "getting good" and then bad again and won't really have learned this lesson until he's given about 1,500 gives on each side. I need to tell you this so you don't get frustrated along the way. The good news is that when you get proficient at recognizing the "give" and releasing immediately, you can get 100-150 "gives" or more every ten minutes or so.

When your horse has learned this lesson, he'll be a safer horse to ride. He'll be thinking back at you more and looking for the "boogey man" less. This lesson is integral to the process of developing a willing attitude in your partner by teaching your horse to recognize your requests and respond to them. 🐾

BOB SAYS:
Horses do go through learning cycles. Don't get frustrated when they enter a bad cycle. Just know that when you work through it, you'll have a better horse!

Don't be Fooled!

Don't be fooled by the horse that turns in the direction of the rein you're using but doesn't "give." We are seeking the "give"; if he turns but doesn't "give," keep holding until he does. If he "gives" but doesn't turn, that's okay for now. Someday, we may even want our horse to "give" to the left while going directionally to the right.

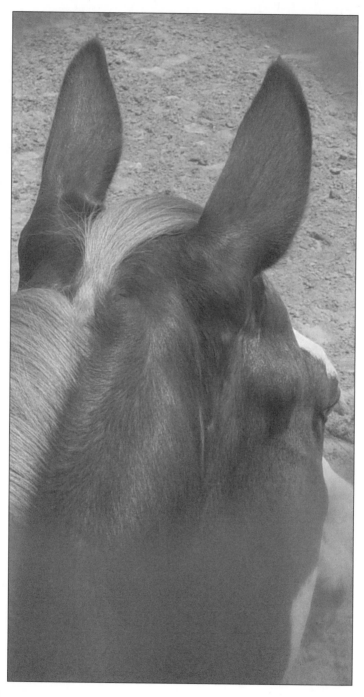

Part 2: The Poll

HERE'S WHERE WE SUPPLE BOTH SIDES OF THE HORSE AND GAIN LATERAL FLEXION

The poll is basically the top of the horse's head just behind the ears. Since we must teach both the right and left sides of the horse, we'll imagine that there are two spots on his poll to control.

Picture two half-dollar size spots, one on each side of the horse's head just below his ears. The left spot must move at least 6 inches to the left when asking with the left rein and vice versa for the right spot. Remember that when the horse moves his jaw in the correct direction, we must release immediately, even if that movement is less than 6 inches.

BOB SAYS:
Use mini-releases to deepen this give — the start of our lateral flexion.

If he moves his poll in response to our cue, say, one inch to the correct side, release quickly, but within two seconds you must ask again. Continue to ask for "gives" using a series of what I call mini-releases. A mini-release is asking for a give again within one or two seconds of the previous give. When he gives, release, then ask again. When he has moved the poll 6 inches or more. At this point, give your horse a complete release (don't ask for anything for at least three seconds).

Eventually, you'll need fewer and fewer requests to achieve that required 6-inch movement. Your horse may even move his poll 6 inches or more with only one give. This is great!

Lateral Flexion

Movement of the horse's poll to the side is lateral flexion. We must get lateral flexion to soften the horse, get him giving and eliminate physical or mental resistance.

Vertical flexion comes much later, once your horse has learned to give completely. We will discuss this in Part 10, page 135.

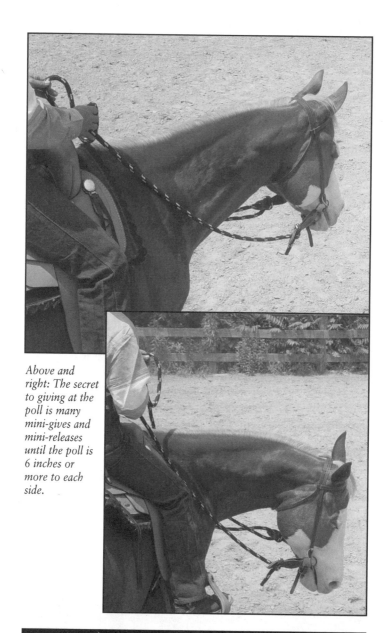

Above and right: The secret to giving at the poll is many mini-gives and mini-releases until the poll is 6 inches or more to each side.

The Release - Again!

Remember: As soon as your horse gives, you must release immediately, then you can ask again! The release is his reward for doing it correctly.

Regardless of the number of "gives" needed to reach 6 inches or more of movement to the side, make sure you release completely when it's there. However, here is where it can get tricky.

Let's say you ask for the horse to "give" to the left and he moves his poll 10 inches in that direction and leaves it there. This would be a good thing, but we can't just let him "hang out" there wondering what we want. If we do, he'll eventually bring his head back to straight on his own. We would have incorrectly taught him that he need only leave it over to the side until he feels like taking it back to center. This would teach him that, in this case, he is the "thinker." We need to ask him to bring his head back before he decides to do it on his own. How do we do this?

If he does leave his head over to the side for more than three seconds, ask him to either "give" again and move further to the same side, or ask for a "give" with the opposite rein to take the head back toward straight ahead. We want to be the partner in control of the position of the poll.

We will eventually want to position his head off to the side and have him keep it there until we ask for something else (most horses will be able to hold this concentration for nine or ten seconds before we might have to touch the rein again).

Why do we want this much movement to the side at this stage of our training? To soften the larger muscles of the neck and also to take away some of the resistance provided by the horse's skeletal system when he's nose-to-tail straight.

This movement will also increase your horse's attention span and he may not only "think" back to you, but may even "look" back at you as if to say, "Is this what you want?" Your release of the rein when he gives says, "Yes, thank you very much!" Remember to teach the lesson on both sides of your horse. ☙

Part 3: The Ears

AFFECT HEAD ELEVATION
AND CALM AN EXCITED HORSE

Once again, we'll start by simply asking our horse to "give" his jaw to one side. If we're working on the right side, we'll keep asking for multiple "gives," rewarding each "give" with a mini-release, until the horse's head is off to the right 6 inches or more and staying there for two or three seconds. We now ask for another "give" or two until we see his right ear drop down so it is level with the top of the horse's withers.

> **BOB SAYS:**
> In this deep give, your horse's head will drop down naturally when you ask it to come this far to the side.

As some horses naturally carry their heads higher or lower according to their specific conformation, we will be satisfied (at this point) if the horse's ears are anywhere in an imaginary 8-inch window around the top of his withers. That means his ears would be at a height level somewhere between 4 inches above to 4 inches below his withers. Remember we must also teach this lesson on both sides of our horse.

A horse usually raises his head when excited so this dropping of the head will help to keep our horse calm and relaxed while learning his lessons. ❧

Above: Use this deeper give to help keep an excited horse calm.

107

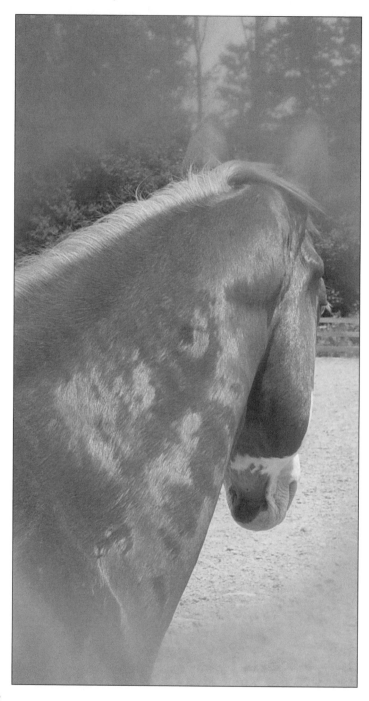

Part 4: The Neck

REPLACE STIFFNESS AND MENTAL RESISTANCE
WITH SOFTNESS AND SUPPLENESS

As the neck is physically a large part of the horse, it is also a large and important element of gaining control. Therefore, we will divide it into three different areas of focus. We'll call them :

A. Long Neck Parallel Pop-Out
B. More Neck Reinbow Arc
C. Great Neck Wrinkle and Crease

> **BOB SAYS:**
> In the beginning, you'll need to actually see the evolution of the neck muscles. But with time, you'll be able to feel for the softness.

You've probably noticed by now that our only job so far has been to ask for the "give" and then release when we get it. We've simply asked with more frequency (less time between requests) and watched as our horse began to give us **Part 2**, page 103 (poll six inches or more off to the side) and **Part 3**, page 106 (ears within eight inch window around withers). Good news! Once again, this is all we have to do.

Now our horse is moving his jaw to the right, his poll is six inches or more off to the right side and his right ear is approximately on an even keel with his withers.

Ask for another "give." You'll see the long muscle in your horse's neck start to move parallel to the ground instead of running "uphill" from the base of his neck towards his ear. As this muscle descends, becoming parallel to the ground, it will also "pop out." Therefore, **Part A** of the neck will be referred to as "**Long Neck Parallel Pop-Out**." When you start to see this consistently within, say, five or six multiple "gives," then teach it on the left side of the horse.

Above: **Long Neck Parallel Pop-Out:** *See how the long neck has popped out in this photo.*

Above: **More Neck Reinbow Arc:** *Look at the nice arc in Lucky's neck from the base of his neck to his ears.*

Now you can return to the right rein and the right side of your horse's neck to start requesting just a little more from the neck. You'll see a huge arc form, starting at the base of his neck going all the way out to his nose. The neck takes on the shape of a rainbow. We'll use a little poetic license here and refer to it as the "**reinbow arc.**" We need to observe this "**More Neck Reinbow Arc**" on both sides of our horse.

Now that we have some tools to work with, it is time to teach the horse to "follow his nose," or go where we point him. It will no longer be acceptable for him to be pointed to the left and moving to the right.

In order to teach this lesson, we'll need two cones placed about 20 feet apart and we'll trot a figure 8 around the cones. Stay at this exercise until it is clear that your horse understands what is expected of him. Obviously, by doing a figure 8, we'll be teaching the lesson to both the left and right sides of our horse. The horse won't learn this lesson at the walk (it's too easy for him) so we must trot this exercise. We don't want him to break gait at any time.

As long as he maintains the gait, we cannot squeeze or kick him continuously. Use as little leg pressure as you can, but as much as you need to get him into the trot, and then assume he will keep this gait until you ask for something else. If he breaks the gait, then "get

his attention" with one or two good kicks from both feet. When he resumes the trot, immediately quit squeezing or kicking. Otherwise, he'll always expect us to kick-kick-kick and will break down the instant we stop kicking. Trotting in this latter case would be more work for us than for the horse and wouldn't be fun for either of us.

During this follow-your-nose exercise, if your horse drifts outside of where he's pointed, hold your rein and squeeze with both legs to "squirt" his motion forward, like squeezing toothpaste out of a tube.

*Left: My whole body is
starting to turn in sync
with my horse's body.*

*Right: Suzanne on
Nack. Her head is
up looking out
where she is going.*

Riding Tips

When you're teaching your horse to follow his nose, you can make it much easier for him to succeed if you are looking where you're going. This sounds simple, but most of us forget and start to look down at the horse's head, or at the ground, which inhibits the horse's movement. Let's help our partner here by using some of our parts in conjunction with his parts.

At the trot, we should be looking 8-10 feet out ahead of us in the direction we want to go. Look with your eyes, obviously, but also point your shoulders, along with your hips, in the same direction. Try to do this an instant before you pick up the rein. Turning your eyes-shoulders-hips, and then using the appropriate rein, will allow your horse to become lighter as he starts to tune into what your body is doing (he will actually start the turn when your eyes-shoulders-hips turn in the direction you are going). It will also help you to avoid leaning into the center of your circles.

112

*Above: **Great Neck Wrinkle and Crease:** You can clearly see the wrinkle and crease in this photo.*

When you're doing the figure 8, remember that all your turns should be part of a circle, nice and smooth. Herky-jerky right angle turns (which could cause your horse to break the gait) are not allowed.

Once our horse is following his nose consistently, we're ready for Part C of the neck. Resume walking and go through Parts 1-3, then **Long Neck Parallel Pop-Out, More Neck Reinbow Arc,** and now one more give should give you control of the base of the neck where it attaches into the shoulders. You'll see some wrinkles form, followed by a crease right at the base which appears like a hinge.

When the horse gives you this **Great Neck Wrinkle and Crease,** you will now have created softness deep enough into the horse's front end to enable you to ask for control of the front feet. ❧

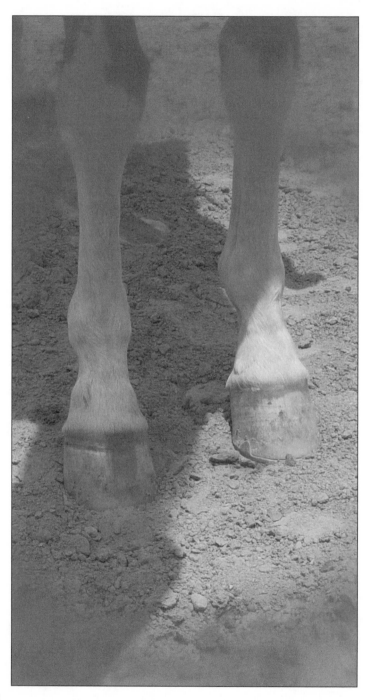

Part 5: The Front Feet

WE CAN NOW ADD CONTROLLED LATERAL AND BACKWARDS MOVEMENT TO OUR REPERTOIRE

When we are consistently able to get Parts 1-4 (pages 97-113), we can now bring into use our *outside* rein to limit how far the horse's head moves to the side and to ask him to "break" at the poll, which we'll define later.

BOB SAYS:
This exercise may seem a bit confusing at first; however, once you get it, you'll benefit from increased control.

Right rein **Left rein**

First, let's start with the analogy of a clock. When we are moving straight ahead, we are moving toward twelve o'clock. When the right front foot steps diagonally to the right, it's moving towards two o'clock; the left front foot steps diagonally to the left towards ten o'clock. A foot moving toward three or nine o'clock would be moving directly to the side and towards six o'clock would be backwards.

We are also going to imagine that the left rein is attached to the right front foot. So, in our mind, the left rein is in our left hand and the other end (the bit end) is connected to the horse's right front foot. You'll use the *left* rein to move the *right* front foot!

Now, pick up the left rein, request "gives" until the wrinkle and crease

Why Do We Need Lateral Movement?

When you are able to achieve lateral movement from your horse, you will have increased control in all that you do with him. Therefore, you'll have more safety when you ride. You will also be able to increase the diameter of a riding circle without losing the arc in the horse's body, move away from an oncoming tree, begin the sidepass or even reverse arc circle.

Left: Here I'm checking for the wrinkles, crease and hollow of **Great Neck.**

Right: Now, I've changed my focus to the left front foot and have asked it to step on 11 o'clock. Your horse can feel you looking at his front left foot and will realize that is the part you are concentrating on.

Left: I'm finishing the exercise by having him follow his nose to the right. Again, we do this so our horse never starts to think that if we pick up the right rein, he's supposed to always move to the left. He should only do that when we are requesting it.

on the left side are visible, add the right (outside) rein in order to "hold" this frame and change your focus to the right front foot. Look at it and try to "pick up" the foot, setting it down to the right side on two o'clock. Although you will, in this instance, be using primarily the left rein to "pick up" the right front foot, your right rein will help hold the frame (the bend in his neck) and guide the horse out on the diagonal step. Looking at the hoof you're trying to "pick up" will cause your weight to shift, and help your eyes, shoulders and hips to ride toward two o'clock, making it easier for the horse to understand your request. As soon as the foot moves in the desired direction, release the rein, but then keep the horse moving forward. We don't want to accidentally teach our horse that if he steps diagonally, he should stop.

Once the horse understands the lesson, we can become more and more subtle with our cues until it looks as if the horse is reading our mind. We only exaggerate our body language in the beginning to help the horse succeed.

Using multiple "gives," soften the neck again until the **Great Neck Wrinkles and Crease** are visible; then ask again. Teach both sides and start with just one step on a diagonal, then add two steps, three steps, etc. When you have mastered all the numbers of the clock by focusing on the front feet, we can move on to **Part 6.**

When teaching this lesson (**Part 5**), it's important to remember that each time we ask the opposite front foot to move diagonally, we must finish the movement by having the horse follow his nose for at least an equal number of steps.

We do this so our horse never starts to think that if we pick up the right rein, he's supposed to always move laterally to the left.

He's only supposed to do that when we are requesting it, and he'll start to "feel" where our reins, our eyes and our body parts are asking him to go.

For example, when using the right rein to direct the left front foot to step laterally to the left on eleven o'clock for two steps, also use the same right rein to turn the horse to the right for at least two steps. In this way, we are once again helping our horse to succeed — not testing him to failure.

We want the softness and all the parts more "out front" (see photo caption, below) because, as we advance in our training, straightness in the horse's body becomes more important. ✿

Left: When I say "out front" I'm referring to the position of the horse's head we'd like to see. The softness and the wrinkle/crease occur while the head is closer to straight forward with less bend in the neck.

Part 6: The Withers
CONTROL OF THE WITHERS ENABLES US TO LIGHTEN THE FRONT END AND CONTROL HIS DIRECTION

The next step in gaining control of our horses is to ask for the withers. Again, we'll imagine a half-dollar size spot on either side of the withers. As we are now deeper into our horse's body, vis-a-vis controlling the parts, we should be able to control a wither spot with each rein. That is to say that we could ask the left side wither spot to move forward, backward, up or down, on a diagonal or to the side with the left rein and vice versa.

BOB SAYS: Teaching or playing with your horse should be fun, so enjoy the journey.

We'll start to ride better as we sit up straight in our saddle without having to lean out the way we did when focusing on the front feet.

You will know when you have complete control over the withers because at that point you will be able to ask your horse

Riding Tips

Don't forget to breathe and imagine that your legs are actually long enough to scrape along the arena surface. This position (looking where you're going and scraping the arena with the bottom of your feet) will put that much sought-after "line" from your ears through your shoulder and hip to your ankle, when viewed from the side. I know most of you have been taught to "keep your heels down," but please imagine that you are "scraping" evenly with toes, ball of foot and heel.

When you rest your foot in the stirrup on the "sweet spot," just behind the ball of your foot, this will keep your ankle loose and able to act as a shock absorber. Your heel will still be down (as you rest your foot in the stirrup), but it will not be in a "locked" position.

Left: I've begun to soften the left side of my horse looking for the wrinkle/crease. Notice how my outside rein restricts the sideways movement of the head.

Right: The horse is about to step toward the right as I am directing the left wither spot to the right.

to stand still and just rock his withers left to right and back again. *You'll be dancing with your partner!*

When we can do the clockwork exercise (see page 115) with the wither points instead of the front feet, this will allow us to ride more correctly. Now it's even more important (after you've been able to see the wither spots move when and where you request them to) to shift your weight around and look with your eyes, shoulders and hips in the direction you wish to go. You'll find you'll need less rein as your horse tunes in more to your body movements. ❧

A 17.2 black, dressage horse named Johnny is one example of a horse who was prematurely taught to break at the poll before he was taught to soften and give laterally. This horse arrived at a clinic with the owner who was obviously rather tentative about getting on. She did, however, cowboy up and mount her horse only to have Johnny come bucking and hopping up the driveway with the owner hanging on for dear life.

I helped her off and asked one of my assistants to get on and just walk the horse, teaching it to "give to the bit" (see pages 97-101.) That is, to move its jaw laterally and to soften its neck. That's the only thing we asked this horse to do. We did this because he had been previously forced to "*give his face vertically*" (see pages 135-137) and hold that position. It's like asking a person to stand against the wall with their heels, butt, head, shoulders and neck touching the wall while staring at their navel. If you hold that position long enough, you'll get a knot or a charlie horse in your neck. That's what was happening to this poor horse, Johnny. He was getting sore. He was forming a "Johnny Horse." And every time he was forced to hold that frame, it hurt. Finally, he just said, "No, I'm not doing that!"

So he did whatever he had to do, whether it was buck, rear, or bolt to relieve the pain the forced position was causing.

Therefore, we simply walked him around and taught him to give to the bit laterally. In about 15 minutes, the owner got back on and proceeded to ride in the clinic. She was so happy with the clinic and the progress that she decided to leave Johnny with us for a couple of weeks to retrain.

Then, I was presenting at a clinic five or so years later in the town Johnny was originally from. I was approached by a veterinarian after one of my lectures. He came over to shake my hand and to congratulate me for helping a horse named Johnny. I didn't remember at first which horse he was talking about but when he said 17.2 black, dressage horse and his lovely, lively and funny owner, I immediately knew. I thanked him but asked why he was congratulating me. He said, "Because you not only helped the horse to be a better horse under saddle, but you also helped him with being groomed, shod and vetted. He is just a better overall horse to handle and be around." To have a vet notice, well, what a surprise that was for me!

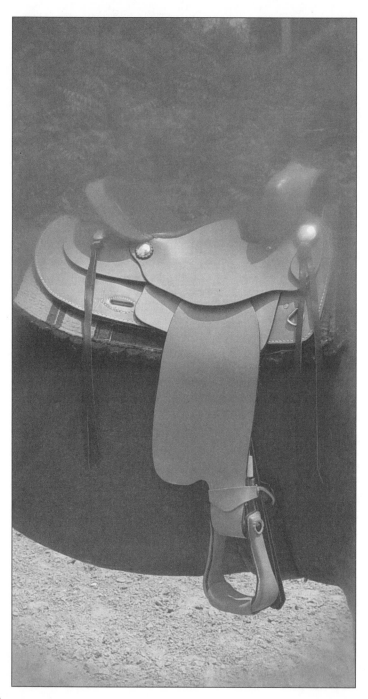

Part 7: The Barrel

TEACH YOUR HORSE TO RESPOND TO YOUR LEG CUES

Because horses do not naturally move away from pressure, it is necessary to teach them to do so. It is easier to do this now that we can control the front feet or the withers with our reins. Continue to perform the lateral work using either the horse's front feet or withers, but now start to add your leg on the side of the horse opposite the direction that he is moving.

For example, if you're using the left rein to direct the right front hoof or left side wither point to move to the right towards two o'clock, also add your left leg to "push" the horse towards two o'clock. When pushing with your left leg remove your right leg to "open" the door on that side.

Eventually the horse should need only a seat and leg cue. Don't feel you need to exaggerate where you place your leg cue. Horses can feel very minute differences in pressure and will eventually recognize the subtle change in our leg placement when requesting the sidepass, diagonal, or turn on the forehand, etc.

This system of teaching leg cues takes far less time than trying to introduce them without first gaining rein control. It also gives you a back-up plan (using the rein) if someday your horse doesn't respond to your leg cue. 🐎

Riding Tips

This large area of the horse is controlled primarily by our legs, which should be draped (not gripping or clutching) along the horse's side as we ride. To ask for movement, a light squeeze with the inside of our calf muscle should be all that is needed.

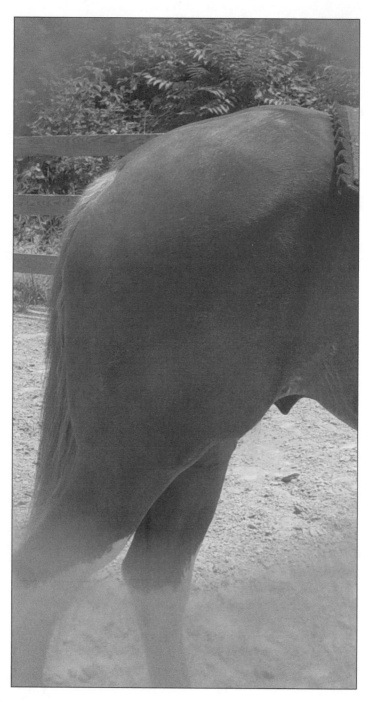

Part 8:
The Hindquarters
CONTROL THE ENGINE AND YOU CONTROL THE HORSE

It is my opinion that, with the exception of the jaw, the hindquarters are the most important part of the horse to control. The hindquarters, comprising the hip and the rear legs, can be referred to as "the engine." This is where impulsion starts; it is the power plant of the horse.

> **BOB SAYS:**
> Control of the hips gives us control of the horse's engine.

If a horse bolts and we are able to disengage his hip and get the rear legs to move sideways, we can effectively shut down the engine and regain control. This is our "emergency stop."

You'll need to practice this movement until it becomes a "muscle memory" for you because what you practice is what you will do in a crisis. When a horse bolts, you don't have a lot

CAUTION from Bob!

Within 10-20 attempts, this movement (disengaging his hindquarters) usually cures horses from bolting if you catch them in the first couple of strides. The longest it ever took me to cure a confirmed bolter was 100 times, the second longest 22 times.

We cannot, or I should say must not, disengage the hindquarters if we allow the horse to achieve a full gallop because we might inadvertently pull him over on top of us. Therefore, it is imperative to disengage that hip within the first one or two strides of a bolt or even when you can feel the horse tighten up as if he is ready to bolt.

125

Left: Suzanne has started to disengage the hip. Notice her left hand moving toward her right shoulder as she looks at the horse's left hip.

Below: This is a shot of the same movement taken from the side.

Left: The horse has completed the movement and has received her release of the rein pressure.

of time to think about what to do. It must become a conditioned response or reflex for us to pick up the rein on the side our horse gives to best, and disengage the hindquarters and get the emergency stop.

To start, walk your horse forward. Pick up the left rein and begin to take the slack out slowly while actually turning your body to look at the point of the horse's left hip. Continue to add pressure on the rein, bringing your left hand diagonally across your torso toward your right shoulder until you see the left hip start to move to the right.

As soon as one hip starts to move in the desired direction, release all pressure on the rein. The rear legs will automatically move with the hip, giving you a distinct feeling of two steps to the right accompanied by a slight rearward shift in the horse's weight. Again, you must also teach this lesson from the right side.

At first, you'll need your horse to just do it, then do it every time you ask, and then, finally, do it "pretty." Sometimes you'll need serious pressure on the rein in order to get our horse to "just do it." However, always start with an "ask." You can gradually increase rein pressure to encourage, insist or even order. As he starts to understand what you're asking, he'll "do it every time." That's when you'll need to work on a slower, lighter rein until he "does it pretty" (responding more quickly on a loose rein).

Remember, when you start teaching this lesson, the horse will have no idea what you're asking him to do. That's why it's important to actually look at the horse's hip when you first ask it to move. That way you will not only feel the movement, you will also see it, which allows you to release your rein pressure immediately. The release tells the horse he gave you the right answer.

Remember, we need to teach the horse on both sides. Now, go through all the steps using the right rein. You now have an emergency stop to help you deal with any attempts at bolting!

TAKE IT ONE STEP FURTHER

BOB SAYS:
Use the hip for more advanced maneuvers like sidepassing or backing the "L" in a trail class.

Now, teach the lesson from a standstill and start applying a leg cue in order to achieve a turn on the forehand. Get one step to the side and release both the rein and leg cues. Build up to two steps before releasing, then three, then four, etc. until you can complete a full 360 degree turn on the forehand. Keep practicing until your horse will do it on your leg cue alone. This will free up your reins to control the front end and prevent it from moving around too much. ⁊

Left: Start with the emergency stop to begin to teach the turn on the forehand.

Right: Here the horse is responding to her leg and Suz uses her reins to hold the front end in place.

Turning on the Forehand

The turn on the forehand is a movement of the horse's hind legs to the side while the front legs remain relatively still. A "complete" turn on the forehand would entail a full 360-degree circle by the hind legs around the front legs.

Sometimes, we get a little too hung up on what is the proper cue to do this or the proper way to get that. I often tell people, "You have to understand that it's more than just one thing that gets the horse to react in the way you want him to."

For example, if you ask someone, "What is the your cue to pick up the left lead in the canter or the lope?" most often they will say, "Well, I put my right leg behind the girth and squeeze." They might add, "I lift the left rein or whatever." That leg cue is pretty universal.

But, if you think about it just for a minute, your right leg cue for the horse to perform the turn on the forehand would then be identical to the cue to pick up the left lead canter.

So just how does your horse know the difference? Is he a mind reader? No. In the case of the left lead canter, we're looking out, our bodies might start to ride the canter with our seat bones moving forward and our energy is up. We've collected the horse and set him back on his rear end a little bit.

In the case of the turn on the forehand, our energy is subdued and we're focusing on moving the hips over, therefore we've weighted his front end. We don't usually think about these things but they happen unconsciously when we think about the single clear intent of either moving the hindquarters over or picking up the left lead canter.

But what I want to get across here is: To the horse, it's all just a picture. It's many little things our body does that presents a picture to the horse of what we want. I believe this is how horses learn. They are masters of body language. A mean face from us when we're asking a horse to come to us will almost guarantee that he won't come to us, while a happy face can convince him to come in. If we want his hip to move away from us and we're smiling at it, it's probably not going to move away. But if we make a nasty face, like the way a mare does when she wants her foal to step aside, we might be able to chase that hip away.

So body language is the language that horses speak. They understand the picture our whole body is giving them. It's not just where our left leg is, or where our hand is, but a combination of all those things which is so important to the understanding your horse has for you.

So when you've been riding a horse for a long time and you think to yourself, "Wow, what a great place for a canter!" and your horse immediately does it, it's not voodoo! It's your body sending out about four thousand little signals telling your horse that is exactly what you wanted.

Bob's Cue to Canter

Incidentally, I don't like to ask a horse to go forward with just one leg. I like to use two legs to get forward motion. To canter, I would use the left leg at the cinch and the right leg behind the cinch. And that would be the position for the horse to pick up the left lead canter.

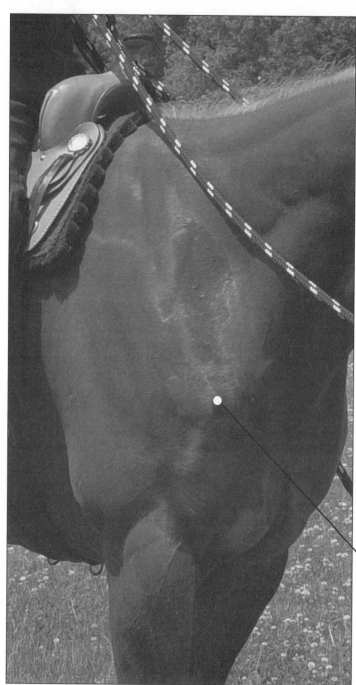

Shoulder
Point

Part 9:
The Shoulder Points

CONTROL OF THE SHOULDER POINTS
FURTHER SOFTENS OUR HORSE, HELPS US
TO BACK UP AND PICK UP SPECIFIC LEADS

We start to gain control of the shoulder points by taking advantage of the movement we achieved in gaining control of the hindquarters. In order to teach both sides of the horse to stop, we can use our control of the hips, together with the shoulders, to begin to teach our horse a correct, balanced stop.

BOB SAYS:
Control of the shoulder points is also where your balanced stops begin.

Repeat the left hip disengagement, release the rein, but then immediately change your focus from the left hip to the left shoulder point. Start to take the slack out of the left rein, increasing pressure slowly until the left shoulder point stops moving forward.

If after disengaging the hindquarters the left shoulder point has already stopped, then do nothing. When the horse is doing it every time (disengaging hip and stopping the shoulder point on the left side), then we can proceed to teach the right side. To repeat the steps:

1. Move the left hip with the left rein to the right, release rein
2. With the same left rein, immediately ask the left shoulder point to stop moving forward, release rein
3. Enjoy the stop; wait at least three seconds before repeating.
4. Repeat on right side.

When we practice these movements enough, the horse will eventually put the movements together. When you pick up the left rein and ask the horse's left hip to move to the right, the

131

Right: Here I'm trying to stop everything at once. Notice how it has affected my position.

Left: I'm focusing on the left shoulder point and asking my horse to stop going forward but to stay soft through his neck and shoulders while doing so.

Below left: And now, I'm just focused on the shoulder points. See how nice the stop becomes.

Right: Now, we're "getting it pretty!"

horse will automatically stop his left shoulder. Please note the feet may move backwards, but this is not necessary. Now what we've just taught on the left side, we must teach on the right as well. Remember to go through the steps using the right rein.

When this has been accomplished, you can eliminate step one (disengaging the hip). Move the horse forward and go directly to asking the left shoulder point to stop. Keep him soft and supple. Then teach the stop from just the right shoulder point. The next step is to keep our horse straight, ask the left shoulder point to stop and, within the very next stride, ask the right shoulder point to stop. Then without a release, simultaneously ask both points to rock backward with both reins.

> **BOB SAYS:** Your leads can also be obtained from the shoulder points.

Again, stop the left shoulder with the left rein and immediately stop the right shoulder with the right rein, then, without a release, ask both shoulder points to rock back using both reins, then release. All we're trying to do here is plant the idea that when he stops, he should shift his weight to the rear.

Eventually we can simply use both reins simultaneously to ask the shoulders to stop and rock backward. As the horse starts to anticipate rocking back after each stop, he will start to bring his hindquarters further up underneath himself in the stop, becoming lighter and more balanced. You no longer need to try to stop your whole horse, you just stop the shoulder points. When you focus on the shoulder points, you will also sit the stop more correctly (see photos left.)

We can also move the shoulder points on a diagonal to the right or left or move them directly to the side or move them backwards just as we did with the front feet and the withers. We're focusing on a different spot but we'll have more control because our horse is giving much deeper in his body. The shoulder point, you see, is just the tip of the iceberg. What we're really controlling is everything from the shoulder point to up under our seat on whichever side of the horse we're dealing with. ❧

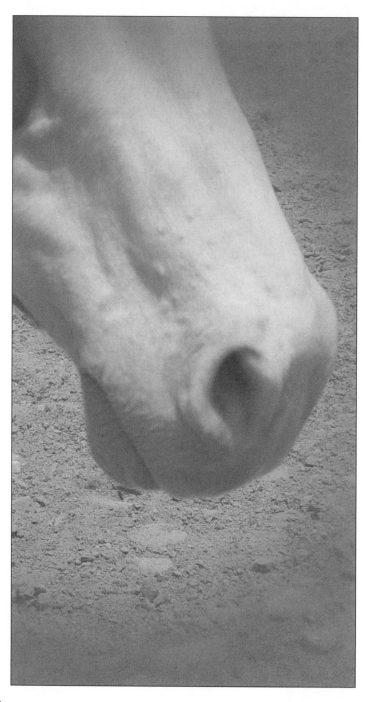

Part 10: The Nose

CONTROL OF THE NOSE IS AN IMPORTANT PART OF COLLECTION

Now we have gained control over the shoulder points and have our horse stopping nicely and rocking back after the stop. Here is where we will ask the horse to stop and, without a release of the rein, ask him to back up for ten steps or until he "breaks" at the poll, whichever first occurs. When either happens, release the rein and let the horse stop for three seconds.

BOB SAYS:
Never push a horse to back up if you think he's going to rear.

Breaking at the poll is also referred to as "coming on the vertical" or "giving his face." These terms all refer to the horse bringing his nose towards his chest until there is a straight line formed from the horse's ears straight down his face through his nose, perpendicular to the ground. It is part of collection; the shoulders will soften and the withers rise as he "breaks." Then you will be able to feel his back round up underneath you.

The reason I tell you to back ten steps is that most horses will not resist ten steps too vehemently. After that, however, a horse that is especially resistant to backing may start to get

Above: This horse has started to back and break at the poll.

135

Above: Here, I have made Blackjac over flex slightly. We'd rather have the horse a bit in front of the vertical than behind it. We don't ever want the horse to evade the bit by over flexing.

Above: This is what we want! You can see the vertical line from the horse's face to the arena surface.

really annoyed, or even begin to rear. You need to release immediately if he breaks at the poll because we never want to punish a horse when he's doing something correctly.

You may have to stop and back your horse those ten steps about thirty times before he breaks at the poll, so don't get frustrated if he doesn't do it right away. When he does start breaking at some point during your ten-step backup, you must release immediately, whether it's on the seventh backward step or the third. Your release tells the horse that the break at the poll is what you were asking for.

Once you feel that he has learned the lesson, you can add steps to your backup while releasing on each correct step. In effect, you stop your horse and ask him to back, he backs a step while breaking at the poll, you release and say "Thank you." Then you ask again saying, "Please continue to back correctly." Your release should be more like a mini-release here because we don't want to lose the horse's backward momentum. If we wait too long to ask we'd have to "pull" on him to back and we really don't want to do this at this stage of our training.

> **BOB SAYS:**
> We want true collection, not just head set.

Limit your correct backup to three steps (releasing on each step) in the beginning because we never want to test to the point of failure. We always want to help our horse succeed. You may gradually increase the number of steps in the backup until eventually you can back the length of the arena with lightness, vertical flexion, collection and straightness.

> **BOB SAYS:**
> Don't ask for too much too soon. When the horse "breaks," you must release even if he then pushes his nose out. Eventually, he'll learn to hold the position by himself.

If your horse has not been trained to break at the poll, his neck muscles will not be ready to hold this position for more than two or three steps at a time. Allow him sufficient time to build up these muscles slowly (*months*, not days). Then you can begin requesting that he *give to the bit and break at the poll in all your forward exercises as well.* ❧

> **BOB SAYS:**
> Allow him months to build his muscles up slowly.

137

Partnership Training
for Horse & Rider

PHASE 3

Training Patterns
to Build on Your
Breakthroughs

Now the fun begins! We will combine all the parts we've learned to control, and perform the exercises in the back of this book. Left: Moving laterally. Below: Backing the "L."

Combining Parts

NOW COMBINE THE PARTS TO DO JUST ABOUT ANYTHING WITH OUR HORSE

Once we can request and receive the use of any part of the horse, we've developed a solid foundation for more advanced maneuvers! This is where we can utilize the "tools" we now have in our "toolbox."

For example, if we want to teach a horse to sidepass, we can use our reins to ask the right front foot to step on 3 o'clock for two steps and then with our leg ask the hip and rear legs to move over for two steps. Ask the front foot again, then the hip, etc. Ask simultaneously with both your reins (front end) and legs (hindquarters) and you're now sidepassing.

BOB SAYS:
Use the parts you've learned to control the sidepass, back the "L," pick up leads and correct problems

We can use the point of the shoulder or the points of the hip to direct our horse while backing the "L" in a trail class. Or if we want our horse to pick up the "right" lead canter, put him in the right lead at the trot by positioning his right shoulder point ahead of the left shoulder point and squeeze him into the canter.

Use both legs to squeeze him into the canter, but start by positioning them for your right lead canter cue (usually right leg at cinch, left leg slightly behind cinch) and eventually all you'll need is the leg cue to achieve the desired lead.

Furthermore, these "tools" can be used to correct problems that may occur. For example, we could cure the horse that bolts or tries to "run out" his shoulder toward the gate by disengaging the hindquarters and squeezing him forward in the direction we want.

As you can see, the knowledge and breakthroughs you've

accomplished will give you the confidence to play with your horse and have some fun together.

Think of new things you want to teach your horse and experiment with your toolbox. It is a great way to create even more breakthroughs as you improve that bond with your partner that we all search for!

RIDING EXERCISES

In order to keep your horse (and you) motivated, I recommend lots of variety in the exercises that you use. Also, try to vary the length of your training sessions, location, venue and tasks. Design your exercises to be engaging and interesting. Stay focused and your rewards will be every bit worth the effort!

The following exercises are designed to incorporate all you have learned into a program that has practical applications in whatever discipline you choose to undertake.

LIST OF EXERCISES
The Straight Line
The Figure 8
The Triangle
Inside-Outside Circle
The Wagon Wheel
Serpentines
Serpentine with Lead Change
The Circle
Backing the "L"
The Sidepass
Circles with Sidepass - Picking up Leads from a Stop or Walk
A First Step to Lead Changes
Flying Lead Change - Two Circles & Straight Line

Round penning is absent from this book for a reason. People need to be taught how to use a round pen correctly before they attempt it themselves. And that is working hands-on with a serious, reputable and knowledgeable round pen trainer. You can't learn from a video or book and not everyone can get the same results a professional can achieve.

If, however, naivete was the worst of round penning pet peeves, then it wouldn't be so bad. Unfortunately, if you don't know what you're doing, you can drive a horse crazy in the round pen. You can get him so confused that he might go through or over the round pen just to get away. The primary reason for these failures is that people don't know when to release the pressure.

And I'll hear people say, "I've been training my horse in the round pen for six months now!" Watch out, this horse is probably numb to any cue that you give in the pen.

Your horse should be trained in the round pen for one week maybe two, but hardly ever more than that. The training is just not progressing well if he needs more than that. And if you see confusion or worse, aggression, get out of the round pen and don't put him back in until you seek a reputable professional to fix the mistakes.

Another thing, you'll often see someone that will work a horse for two or three hours until he is dripping with sweat. The horse's head is just about two inches from the ground and his rib cage is about to explode. Then they put a saddle on and say, "Look what a great job I've done breaking this horse!" Well, you "broke" that horse all right. You can get on him today, but tomorrow he won't be so tired. The intent of good round pen training should never be to get the horse so tired that he doesn't care what you do anymore.

There is also a myth about round penning. Some people say, "I don't want my horse round penned, even by a knowledgeable and renowned horse trainer, because then I'll never be able to lunge. Every time I send him out, he'll turn in and face me!"

Well, that may be true if the round pen work was done improperly. Properly done, it's just like proper lungeing. Your horse should know when you invite him in to face you, and when you don't he should stay out on the circle. This is a matter of proper versus improper training.

The intent of good round pen training is to give the horse a choice so that he can figure things out for himself; not through punishment and scorching of his lungs, but through a release of pressure on the right answer and a non-release of pressure — not an escalation of pressure — when he gets the wrong answer. Most horses will eventually figure it out and a good trainer will do it without exhausting a horse. You should be able to get a horse to "turn and face you" in less than an hour. Once you've taught the horse something well in the round pen, you will probably never have to use the round pen again.

143

The Straight Line

Since the shortest distance between two places is a straight line, we must teach our horses to walk that way. Horses don't naturally walk in straight lines; they meander aimlessly if left to their own devices. So tack up your horse and ride him someplace where you can focus on two cones or some other points of reference. Line them up one behind the other. Both objects must be aligned for you to recognize when you go off course.

Start by walking the horse forward on the straight line, but then drop the reins "on the buckle" or onto the horse's withers.

> **BOB SAYS:**
> This exercise teaches the horse to stay between your legs and your reins.

As soon as the horse veers off (and he will), pick up the appropriate rein to redirect his nose back to the straight line. When his nose goes back to the straight line, release the rein and place it back on the withers.

He'll probably cross over the line in the other direction. When he does, redirect him back to the straight line. This exercise will resemble a drunken sailor as you start. As you progress in the exercise, your horse will veer less and less until eventually he'll walk it perfectly. He'll learn that if he stays going where you have pointed him, you will leave the reins alone. Remember when you must redirect his nose back on track, you want a "give" from him. Make sure you don't "pull" him around. When you have this exercise solid at the walk, move up to a trot and, eventually, a canter. 🐎

> **BOB SAYS:**
> Small orange traffic cones are helpful in all these exercises. They are pliable and won't hurt if stepped on.

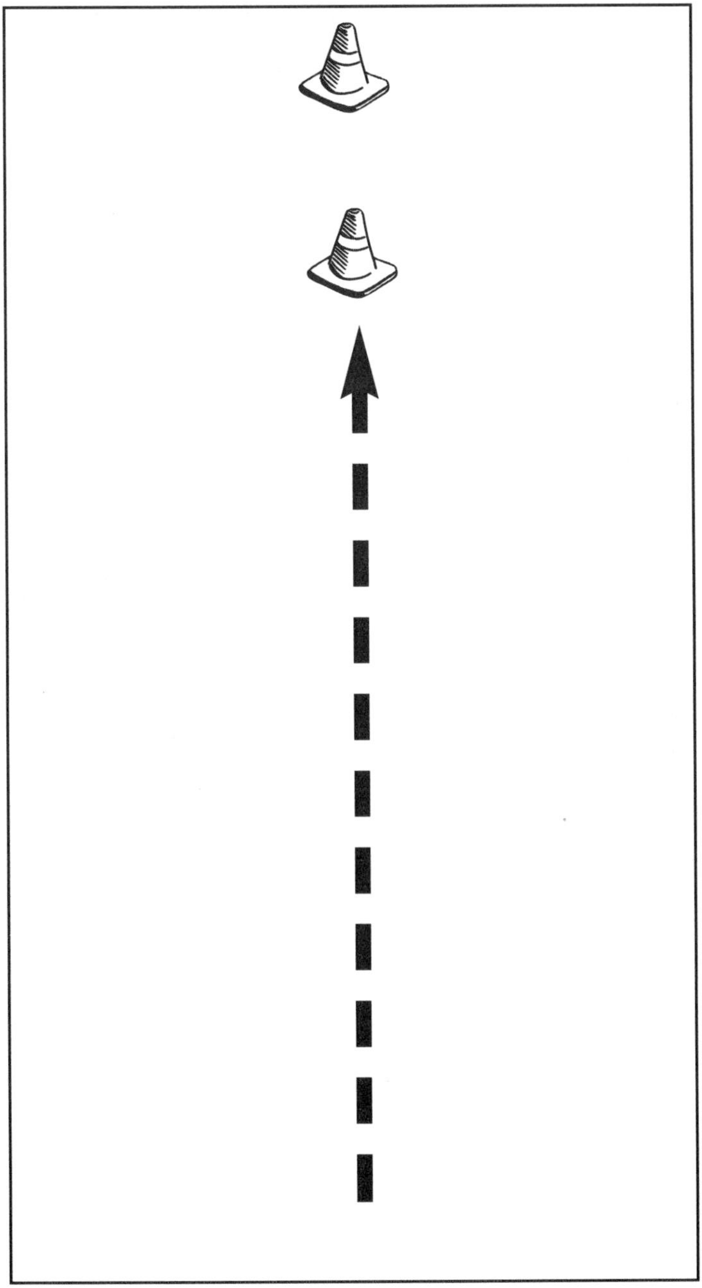

The Figure 8

A great exercise to teach your horse to follow his nose or go where he's pointed is the figure 8. Place two cones as visual references approximately 20 to 30 feet apart. Think of riding a circle around each cone, separately, rather than thinking of a figure 8. This will help you to ride a more correct circle and it will be easier for your horse to maintain an arc in his body that matches the size of the circle, helping him to balance.

> **BOB SAYS:**
> Try to ride this exercise without leaning into the circle; stay centered on your horse.

Circle one cone going to the left and circle the other cone going to the right. Don't let him break into a trot if you're walking and don't let him break down to the walk if you're trotting. We want to control which gait our horse performs in; this should not be his decision.

Don't nag the horse with constant bumping of your legs or feet; instead, ask once for the trot and leave him alone. You must allow him to make the mistake of breaking down rather than attempting to keep him going when you *think* he might be likely to break the gait. Only if he does break down may you apply your "move" cue.

If you nag continuously, your horse will always need a constant bumping to keep going. Then moving forward on him becomes more work for you than for your horse.

Start the exercise at a walk and move up to the trot as soon as possible because the lesson truly needs the trot in order for it to sink in. ❧

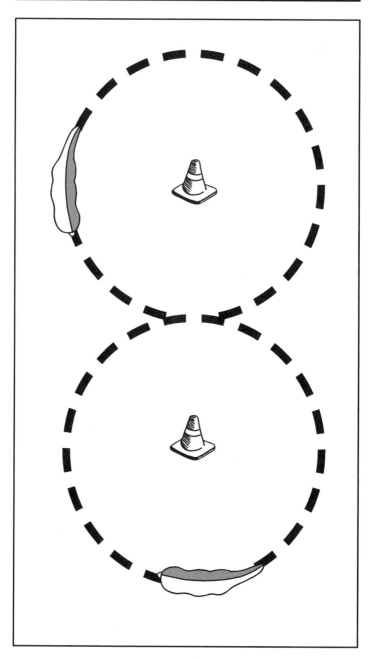

The Triangle

In order to practice moving on a sideways diagonal with precise control, try the Triangle exercise.

Place three sets of cones (six cones in total) approximately 30 feet apart in a triangular shape and keep each individual pair about 3 feet apart.

Ride your horse through the first pair of cones while keeping him straight as you enter into the triangle.

Begin to soften the left side of your horse, asking him to give to the bit, break at the poll and have his right front foot step on one o'clock for several continuous strides into and through the second set of cones.

> **BOB SAYS:**
> You can do this exercise by controlling the front feet, the wither points or the shoulder points. Try all three ways to see the difference.

Now as you pass through this second pair of cones, without changing the arc in the horses body, have him "follow" his nose to the left completing a half circle which will take you through the third and final set of cones. Go straight through and set your horse up for another try.

This next try will be in the opposite direction. Go straight through the first set of cones, soften up the right side, have the horse drift left with the front feet stepping on eleven o'clock going through what was our final set of cones on the last go. Have him continue through these cones, following his nose to the right (again, without losing the arc in his body) and through the remaining set of cones.

When you can do this well at the walk, take it up to the trot and repeat this exercise in both directions. Canter this exercise only when you're doing very well at the trot. ❧

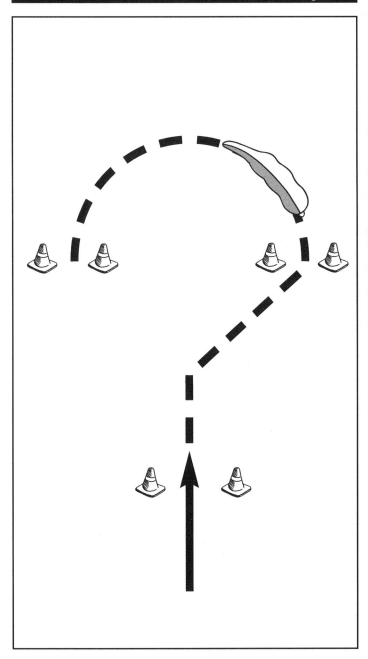

Inside-Outside Circle

This is a wonderful exercise for teaching riders to have "quiet" hands.

Place cones in a 40-foot circle and trot outside the circle going to the left using only your left rein to steer. If (and more likely when) your horse comes inside the circle, remember you're not allowed to redirect him with the right rein. You've learned that you've oversteered your horse.

Try again, staying a little further out from the cones. When you're able to do two or three circles without coming inside the cones (without using the right rein), then start to add an outer circle of cones approximately 10 feet further out than your original circle. Continue to ride outside the original set of cones, but now also stay inside the outer circle of cones.

> **BOB SAYS:**
> Constant changing and readjusting of reins from right to left and back again annoys horses more than just about anything else. This lesson corrects that problem.

Gradually bring the outer cones closer and closer to the original cones until there is only 3 feet between the inner and outer circles of cones. When you can do this, you'll have learned how little rein you actually need if you focus on where you're going. Look in the direction of travel, give your horse proper preparation time and allow him to stay between the reins and your legs. Now try the complete exercise over again, this time to the right using only the right rein.

When you are doing this well in both directions at the trot, repeat the exercise at the canter, again in both directions.

&

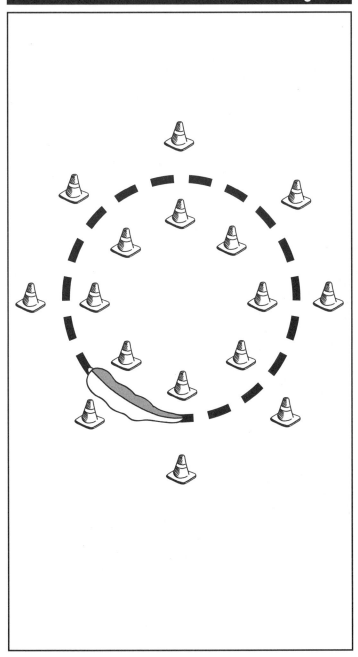

The Wagon Wheel

This is the best single exercise I know of because it accomplishes so much for both horse and rider. It is a trotting exercise, although you may want to walk through it once or twice. You'll need nine cones or other points of reference. Start with a center cone and then make a circle with a diameter of approximately 40 or 50 feet using the other eight cones.

Start by trotting across the center of the circle and pick a spot between any two cones to exit the circle. When you do, begin to circle the cone to your right until you re-enter the circle between the two adjacent cones. Go straight past the center cone and pick a spot between two cones on the other side to exit the circle again. This time circle the cone to your left until you re-enter the circle, again pass the center cone and pick a new exit point on the opposite side. Keep repeating, right circle around one cone, then left circle around a cone on the other side; keep changing your entry and exit points.

BOB SAYS:
This is my favorite exercise. All horses and students in my training program spend many hours working on this.

This exercise has many variations and you can change the priorities according to the lesson you are teaching. It's a great exercise to teach your horse to follow his nose, maintain his trot without breaking into the walk, slow down a runaway trot, balance in his circles, drift out or in on cue, move away from leg pressure and more. It will teach riders to focus, transition, stay upright on turns, maintain proper circles, have light and quiet hands, and incorporate leg and seat cues and more.

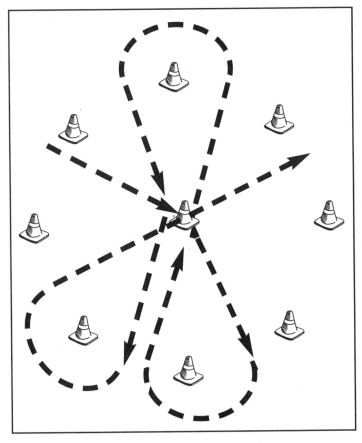

Keep in mind the following points when performing this exercise:

1. Follow his nose where it is pointed.
2. Maintain speed at the trot.
3. Keep a nice arc in the horse's body equal to the half circle you are riding.
4. Give to the bit continuously.
5. Get a break at poll while continuing to move forward.
6. Keep your transitions from left to right smooth and vice versa.
7. Keep your lines straight when going across the center line. ❧

153

Serpentines

For variety in your lessons and instead of wearing a rut along the fence line of your arena, try doing a series of serpentines as you traverse the arena.

Start out trotting a straight line and then ask your horse, as you enter your first half circle to the right, to give to the bit, break at the poll, soften up and arc his body from nose to tail on the line of the half circle. Complete the half circle right, ride a straight line across the arena, and then go through all the steps again only this time doing a half circle to the left.

BOB SAYS:
Get off the rail! Serpentines prevent the fence line from steering your mount.

This exercise works both sides of your horse, combines straight lines with half circles and helps him to stay soft through the transitions from right to left to right and back again, all while giving to the bit. 🎋

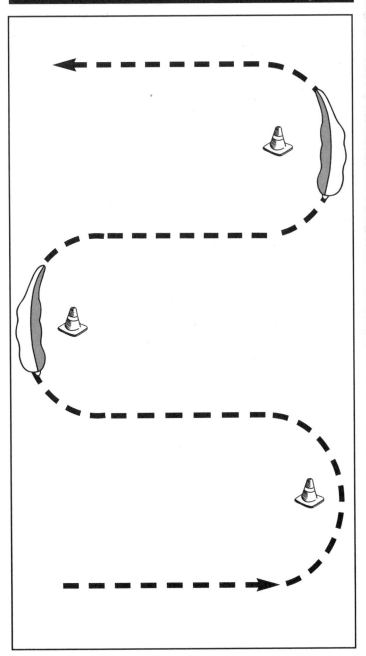

155

Serpentine with Lead Change

Now that we can travel straight lines and perform half circle direction changes, we can add the canter and specific leads.

Begin by trotting your horse across the arena in a straight line. As you approach the turn, show him he's going to the right by looking in that direction and pointing his nose in that direction. Position your left leg just behind the cinch (your right leg remains at the cinch) and squeeze with both legs to obtain the right lead canter. Canter around for half a circle and start going straight across the arena. When you're about half way across, transition down to the trot. As you approach the other side of the arena, begin to turn left and request the left lead canter (right leg behind cinch and the left leg remains at the cinch, squeeze with both legs). Keep repeating as you traverse the arena in both directions. ❧

BOB SAYS:
To prepare your horse for the transitions, both up and down, you can flex your abdominal muscles which will rotate your seat bones. This encourages your horse to engage his hindquarters.

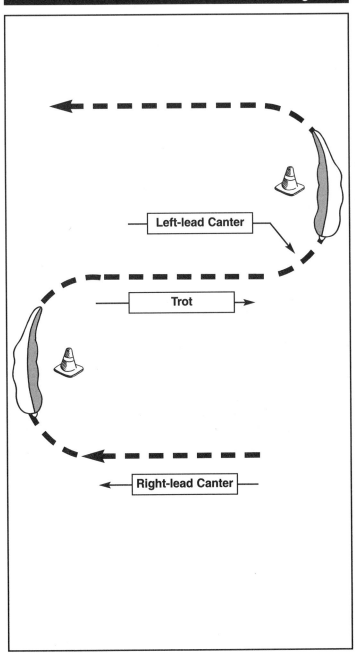

Left-lead Canter

Trot

Right-lead Canter

The Circle

Circling is self explanatory; however, we should know why circles are so important. At the walk or trot, it teaches the horse that he can balance himself quite easily even with us on his back. Practicing at the canter or lope reinforces this fact.

It is of primary importance here that we do not lean into the circle. By leaning in, we are dropping our shoulder (and if we are doing this our horse will most likely drop his shoulder as well) making it difficult for our horse to balance. We want a nice arc in his body with his nose, barrel and tail all touching the line of the circle.

Bigger circles are easier for our horse to canter so start off with an absolute minimum diameter of 60 feet, but know that 80 to 100 feet would be even better. Every time our horse takes his nose off the line of the circle, put it back with a "give" to the bit.

When you have the required impulsion and your horse is giving nicely, you may add the request to break at the poll and ride with collection. ❧

> **BOB SAYS:**
> Remember to release when the horse gives or breaks at the poll. Don't hold him in the desired frame. In time, he will seek the "frame" where he gets released. Voila, self carriage!

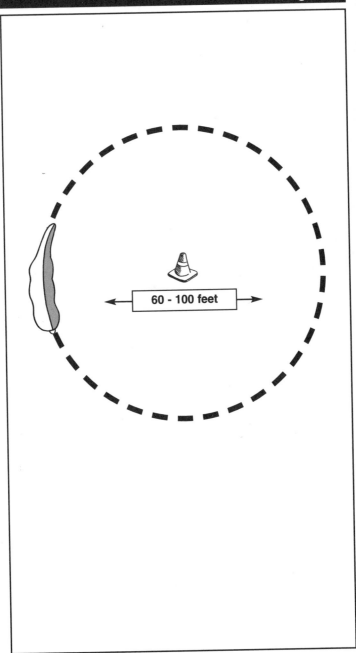

60 - 100 feet

159

Backing the "L"

By now we know that horses can't see directly behind themselves and backing while under saddle, toward poles, fences, or any obstacle does require a modicum of trust in the rider. To back the "L," we'll need not only this trust, but the ability to control the shoulders and/or the hindquarters.

Begin by riding your horse into the "L" between the poles and up to the end line; stop and relax. Then start to back him in a straight line slowly and deliberately. When you believe the time is right, ask either his hindquarters or his shoulders or use a combination of both to move into a 90 degree turn (in the photo in the diagram, the hindquarters would be asked to move to the left and the shoulders would be asked to move to the right). When you are properly repositioned, again ask your horse to back in a straight line while controlling each step.

> **BOB SAYS:**
> This is a great exercise to check how good our leg cues are. If they are not up to speed, we can always use our reins.

Speed is never a consideration in this exercise; we are looking for a controlled step-by-step approach. This exercise is included in almost every arena trail class because we often find ourselves in a similar situation when out in the woods. ᵔ

The Sidepass

After we've gained control of our horse's feet and we are able to have him step on either 3 o'clock or 9 o'clock (see page 115) and move his hindquarters, we can use our reins and leg cues simultaneously to combine these two movements into the sidepass. The sidepass is required in most arena trail classes and is used when opening or closing gates.

To refine the sidepass, we'll get our horse to sidepass the length of an 8-foot pole without stepping forward or backward, keeping the pole under his belly throughout the movement and crossing the outside legs in front of the inside legs.

We'll begin by desensitizing our horse to the pole by walking and subsequently trotting over it until our horse is comfortable with it. Once this is accomplished, ask your horse to step over the pole at the pole's extreme right end and stop with it directly under his belly, just behind where your leg normally hangs. Ask the horse to now sidepass to the right (you should be off the pole with only one step to the side). Praise your horse and approach the pole

> **BOB SAYS:**
> You'll help your horse to be successful if you concentrate on having clear intent to move to the side.

again and step over it, stopping with his belly directly over it as before; however, this time you'll be 6 inches from the end of the pole. Relax and sidepass off the pole (this time it should take only two steps to clear the pole). Continue this exercise adding 6 inches at a time until you reach 2 feet. Then, you'll add 1 foot at a time to the distance the horse must sidepass. Finally, you will be able to approach and stop on the extreme left side of the pole, continuing to sidepass to the right over the entire length of the pole and off. Once you have mastered this movement to the right, start the process over again going in the opposite direction (to the left). Note: Remember to try to keep the horse thinking "forward," which will have him crossing the left legs in front of the right legs when sidepassing to the right, and

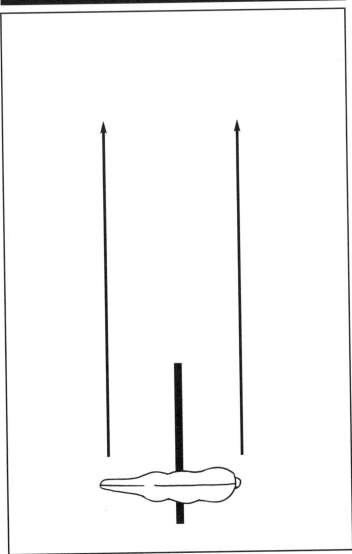

avoid allowing your horse to back up. If he starts to anticipate the movement (i.e. he immediately starts to sidepass when you stop him over the pole), then mix the exercise up with simply walking forward over the pole. ❧

Circles with Sidepass

PICK UP LEADS FROM A STOP OR WALK

This exercise helps teach your horse to pick up specific leads from the walk or the stop. Begin in the center of your arena and pick up a left lead canter while circling to the left in a 70- or 80-foot diameter circle. When you complete a full circle and are again in the center of the arena, stop your horse, relax for a second or two and then side pass two or three steps to the right. This maneuver will result in your horse having a slight bend to the left in his body causing his right shoulder to be the leading shoulder. Immediately request a right lead canter departure and ride a 70- to 80-foot diameter circle to the right. Again stop in the center, relax and sidepass to the left and immediately ask for a left lead canter and so on.

> **BOB SAYS:**
> Please note you can vary this activity depending on the horse's level of training.

If your horse should pick up the incorrect lead, don't jam him with the reins to make him stop. Instead ask for a give to the bit in the direction you are traveling (i.e., if you are circling right and your horse is in the left lead, ask for a give to the bit to the right) and keep asking while gradually making your circle smaller and smaller in diameter. This is hard work for the horse, counter cantering while making their circle smaller and smaller. He will eventually break down to a trot. When he does, begin the circle over and try again.

Note: When your horse is better at recognizing specific lead leg cues, you can reverse the direction of the sidepass, thereby positioning his inside hind more properly to initiate the lead from the hindquarters; i.e., after loping the circle to the left, stop and sidepass left and then cue for the right lead canter to the right. (This is a more advanced canter or lope departure.) ❧

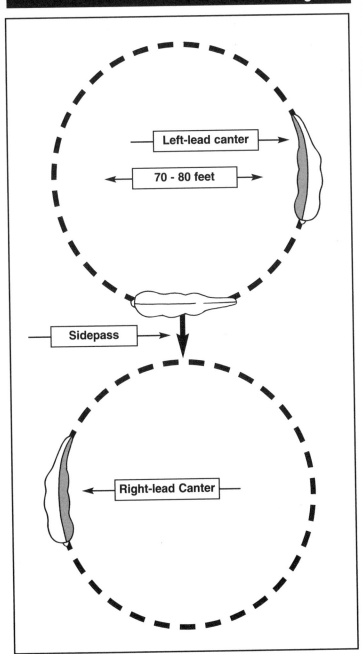

Left-lead canter

70 - 80 feet

Sidepass

Right-lead Canter

165

A First Step to Lead Changes

This exercise allows our horse to make the flying lead change by himself while we're on his back. If you're riding at the canter and you wish to change directions without dropping to the trot or counter cantering, you'll need to introduce your horse to a flying lead change. The best way, in my opinion, to teach this while under saddle with rider is by encouraging him to do it on his own.

Begin by cantering in your horse's least favorite lead (we'll assume this is in the right lead) and go down the long side of the arena and across the short side. Then go diagonally across the center toward the opposite corner of the arena and when you get halfway there, pick up speed. As you approach the corner (at approximately 20 - 30 feet away), show your horse that you are about to turn left (accomplish this by looking to the left and directing his nose to the left with your reins) and allow him to make the change whenever he desires.

> **BOB SAYS:**
> Some horses will change leads with their front legs first in this exercise and change in the rear one stride later.

Note: We've made it easier for the horse to succeed by having him gain speed which helps him change behind and by letting him change to his preferred lead. A failure to change is probably due to lack of speed or a poor diagonal across the arena. ❧

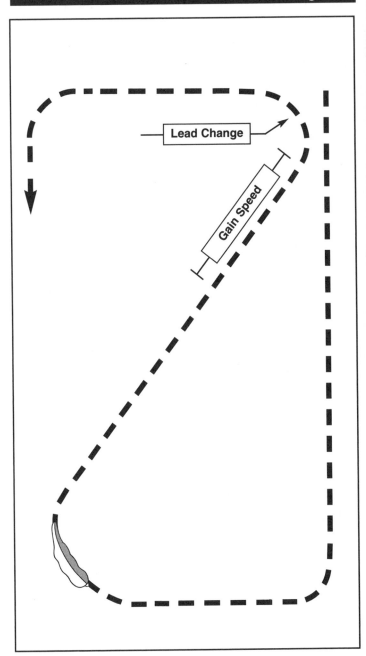

Lead Change

Gain Speed

Flying Lead Change

Once our horse is comfortable changing leads at the canter with us aboard, we can work on giving him the cue to do it where and when we ask. There are several ways to do this, but I'll give you my favorite because I believe it's also easier for the horse. We'll be riding two circles (preferred diameter to begin with is 60 to 80 feet) joined by an imaginary straight line.

Start by circling left in the left lead. When you almost complete the circle and begin the straight line, transition down to the trot across the center, and when you reach the end of the straight line pick up the canter to the right in the right lead. Circle until you again reach the straight line, break down to the trot and at the end of the straight line pick up the canter to the left in the left lead.

> **BOB SAYS:**
> You may also consider placing a ground pole at the spot where you'll ask for the lead change. Sometimes this helps horses to elevate a little longer for the change.

As you continue this exercise, you'll canter on the straight line for a few feet before trotting and you'll ask for the opposite lead canter a few feet before you reach the end of the straight line.

Continue to decrease the trotting time on the straight line gradually until you eliminate it completely. As you approach the center of the straight line, wait for the current leading front foot to land, and shift your weight slightly away from the new direction you wish to go while looking in your desired direction and cue your legs accordingly. When you ask at this time, the horse is about to go into suspension (all four legs off the ground) and he can have an easier time of changing leads behind first. 🌢

168

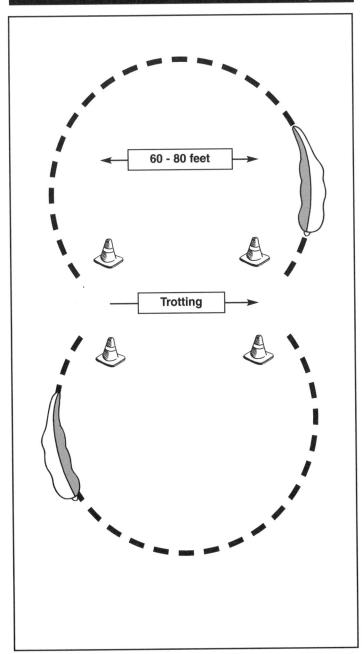

60 - 80 feet

Trotting

169

Closing Comments

I really hope you have enjoyed reading my book and that the ideas and insights presented will help you make incredible breakthroughs in your relationship with your horse.

Horses are wonderful animals and, for the most part, they're willing, mindful and respectful. They are also much bigger, stronger and faster than we are. It's important, therefore, that you always consider safety. There's a little voice inside all of us that warns against doing something dangerous. For the sake of your safety, always listen to your inner voice.

Please be thoughtful and help your horse to succeed, don't test him to the point of failure. Make an effort to keep the fun in your training time by varying exercises and routines. Ride the trails as well as the arena.

Remember to expect improvement, but not every day. Advancement in training slows down as you attempt higher level performance maneuvers. Keeping a diary will help keep you focused on your goals and realistic in your expectations. Perhaps when you need it most, this written record will be useful to see just how far you've already come and what goals you've accomplished.

Building a true partnership takes time. Although it certainly would be nice if it could be accomplished in an hour or two, we both know that when it comes to horses, nothing takes an hour or two. Try to think of the entire process as a work in progress, a journey if you will. Take your time and enjoy the journey.

Bob Jeffreys

Create Your Own Training Diary

Feel free to photocopy these pages for your own use.

Date: _____

Goal: _____

Starting point:_____

_____

_____

_____

Lesson plan:_____

_____

_____

Time spent: _____

Any deviations?_____

_____

_____

Problem:_____

How did you correct the problem? _____

_____

How did the lesson end?_____

_____

Horse's attitude/willingness:_____

_____

Outcome: _____

Create Your Own Training Diary

Feel free to photocopy these pages for your own use.

Date: _____

Goal: _____

Starting point:_____

_____

_____

_____

Lesson plan:_____

_____

_____

Time spent: _____

Any deviations?_____

_____

_____

Problem:_____

How did you correct the problem? _____

_____

How did the lesson end?_____

_____

Horse's attitude/willingness:_____

_____

Outcome: _____

Attend a Bob Jeffreys Clinic

Anyone interested in learning more about horses should attend a Bob Jeffreys Clinic or demonstration with Bob and Suzanne. His down-to-earth, no-nonsense approach to horsemanship is easy to understand and is presented in a clear, unpretentious and often humorous way. Bob has worked with thousands of horses and their partners from the United States, Europe and Iceland. His methods apply to all breeds and disciplines.

Beginners or first-time horse owners will be empowered by the wealth of knowledge they'll learn in a short period of time. Longtime horse owners, riders and trainers will make breakthrough progress with unique yet common-sense, solutions to problems they face and innovative new ways to enhance performance. After all, life's too short to try to learn it all alone and it's more fun in a group.

▶ **Sign up for a clinic:** Check the clinic schedule and sign up online at www.bobjeffreys.com. Click on clinic schedule or call to register.
  - Foundation Clinics
  - Extended Foundation Clinics
  - Advanced Clinics
  - Horsemanship Breakthrough Weeks
  - Kids' Clinics
  - "Sky's the Limit" for Therapeutic Riding Centers
  - Trainer Education Programs

▶ **Host a clinic:** Facilities looking to host a Bob Jeffreys' clinic may inquire online.

▶ **Special Requests:** "Special request" events customized to your training or riding needs.

▶ **Equipment:** Complete selection of recommended products (books, videos, rein kits, etc.) at the tack shop on his website.

To order more copies, photocopy this page and mail it to the address below or save freight and stop by your favorite tack or feed store to pick up a copy!

Yes! I want to order more books. Please send me:

QTY:

___ **It's All About Breakthroughs.** $16.95

___ **Anyone Can Draw Horses.** A 40-page book that will teach anyone to draw horses. $7.95

___ **Trickonometry:** The Secrets of Teaching Your Horse Tricks. $23.95

___ **The Original Book of Horse Treats.** A cookbook of treats and things you can make for your horse. $19.95

___ **The Ultimate Guide to Pampering Your Horse.** Hundreds of pampering tips and helpful hints to please your horse. $24.95

___ **The Incredible Little Book of 10,001 Names for Horses.** Literally thousands of names for horses and ponies. $8.95

___ **Horse Lover's Birthday Book.** A book of days to remember as well as a guide to gifts for horse and humans you can make yourself. $4.95

Add $4.95 for shipping and handling per order. Pay only one price for shipping, no matter how may books you order.

Total enclosed: $_____ (Check, money order, or credit cards accepted. NY residents, please add sales tax.)

Mail to: Horse Hollow Press, PO Box 456, Goshen, NY 10924
Or call: 800-414-6773 to order.

Name:_____

Address:_____

City/State/Zip:_____

Phone:_____

Visa/MC/AMEX:_____Exp._____

Signature:_____

www.horsehollowpress.com